Healing Rain

Revelation from God's
Divine Healing Generals

By John G Lake, Smith Wigglesworth,
and Maria Woodworth-Etter

GodSounds

" Where Faith is Heard"

More books available:

Heavenly Authority: The Right of the Believer by John G Lake

Divine Healing by John G Lake

Spiritual Gifts: What God Gives to Us by Smith Wigglesworth

The Faith Collection: Three Books in One by Smith Wigglesworth

Intimacy with Jesus by Madame Guyon

Words from the Almighty by William S. Crockett Jr.

Polycarp's Letter to the Philipians & His Martyrdom by St. Polycarp

Finney Gold: Words that Helped Birth Revival by Charles Finney

Walking with God by George Whitefield

Looking to publish your own book? Or need your book made into an audiobook? Go to GodSounds.com

To Leila and Mayah, may the Lord use you
to bring His healing virtue everywhere you go.

CONTENTS

CHAPTER 1

I Will Work and Who Shall Hinder?
by *Maria Woodworth-Etter*

Acts 23:9 if a spirit or an angel hath spoken to him, let us not fight against God.

1 Cor 12:4, 7-9 Now there are diversities of gifts, but the same Spirit.....But the manifestation of the Spirit is given to every man to profit withal. For to one is given by the Spirit the word of wisdom; to another the word of knowledge by the same Spirit; To another faith by the same Spirit; to another the gifts of healing by the same Spirit;

1 Kings 8:11 the priests could not stand to minister because of the cloud: for the glory of the Lord had filled the house of the Lord.

1 Sam 12:18 and all the people greatly feared the Lord and Samuel.

1 Cor 2:5 That your faith should not stand in the wisdom of men, but in the power of God.

1 Cor 14:26 when ye come together, every one of you hath a psalm, hath a doctrine, hath a tongue, hath a revelation, hath an interpretation. Let all things be done unto edifying.

I WENT TO SUMMITVILLE, INDIANA and commenced meeting on Wednesday evening Feb. 25, 1885. The house was crowded the first night. The crowd was made up of infidels, sceptics and scoffers. Many of these scoffers were church members. A few of God's children stood by me praying for victory. Most everyone said, she will make a failure here, and were hoping it would be a failure. I went in the strength of God knowing that He that was for me, was more than those who were against me. I arose and told them that God was coming in power; that many of them would be at the altar that night, crying for mercy. I saw some laughing, as if to say, you do not know us. I commenced singing, "Let me in the lifeboat." The Holy Ghost fell upon me. God made them to see the lifeboat on the ocean of eternity, and them drifting away into darkness and despair, down to an awful hell. I led in prayer. When I arose, the silence of death reigned over the house. They were trembling under conviction. While I was preaching, God sent every word like arrows, dipped in the blood of Jesus, to their hearts.

After preaching, I called for sinners to come forward. There was a rush for the altar. It was soon crowded. Those who had opposed me most were the first to come. Some who would not yield were stricken down as dead in different parts of the house. There were many bright conversions the first night. The work went on increasing in interest for one week. About five hundred were saved in the church. The seats were taken out to make standing room. The whole house was a mourners' bench. Many of the worst men in the town and country were saved, and lived earnest Christian lives. Many were saved at home, all around the country, in nearly every house. Some died praising God. Several went out preaching the Gospel. Hundreds have been brought to Christ by their labours.

I commenced meeting at nine o'clock in the morning and closed at twelve at night. Some men arranged to come and break up the meeting. I did not know them, nor what they were doing. They came and crowded in at the door. God pointed the leader out to me. With a loud voice I called to him to come to Christ. The fear of God fell upon him. He turned pale as death and started for the altar. When he got half way he fell under the power of God. He lay about sixteen hours. The way he talked, and his gestures while lying there, brought the fear of God on all who saw him.

Those who came in with him, saw it was a fearful thing to fight against God. (If a spirit or an angel hath spoken to him (Paul), let us not fight against God. Acts 23:9). They were soon on their knees crying for mercy. When he came out he had a wonderful experience to tell, which God used to bring many to Christ. He went to work to bring souls to Christ, and soon began to preach. Many ministers came and received the anointing power from on high. The power of the Holy Ghost fell upon me the first meeting and remained while I was there. It could be seen, heard and felt by all who came. Many times the power would take control of me when singing, praying and preaching. I would be held standing, a spectacle for men and angels. Sometimes I would lie for hours at a time. The holy fire went into all the churches and spread for miles. Hundreds of lost souls were brought to Christ after I had gone to other fields.

From Fairmount we went to Columbia City, Indiana, and commenced meeting in the Universalist Church Thursday evening, March 12, 1885, which lasted about four weeks. Sinners came to the altar the first night. Many made a start for heaven. The interest was so great we engaged the large skating-rink, which was crowded. The interest continued till the last. Many who had been saved in my meetings a year previous, and some of the ministers and Christians who assisted me in those different places, came up to the help of the Lord against the mighty.

CALLED TO PREACH DIVINE HEALING

The Lord showed me while here that I had the gift of healing and of laying on of hands for the recovery of the sick. (Now there are diversities of gifts, but the same Spirit...But the manifestation of the Spirit is given to every man to profit withal. For to one is given by the Spirit, to another the gifts of healing. 1 Cor. 12:4, 7.9.) I had been working day and night for many months and had no strength only as God gave me each meeting. It would be two o'clock often before I would get to sleep. When God began to show me I must preach divine healing I could not understand that it was the Spirit of God leading me. For three nights when I was almost dead for want of rest I lay awake. God was teaching me a lesson I could not, or would not learn. I said: Lord, you know I started out to win souls for heaven, and I have been busy all the time. I have tried to be faithful in everything you have given me to do. I am so exhausted with constant labour that I have to be helped many times to rise from my bed.

I thought if I would preach divine healing they would bring all the cripples in the country, and I would neglect the salvation of souls. The Lord showed me He would take care of the work. I told the Lord if He wanted me to pray for the sick to send them to the meetings, and show me He wanted me to pray for them, and I would. When I made this promise I had perfect rest of mind and soul. From this time God began to lead me to teach divine healing and pray for the sick. It is now nine years since, and God has healed thousands of all manner of diseases. Thousands have been brought to Christ by seeing the people healed. The devil tried to make me think there would not be nearly so many saved.

On Friday, April 10, 1885, we left Columbia City for Hartford City, Indiana. At Fort Wayne we were met by Lawyer C., of Hartford City, who escorted us to his house. In the evening we met the Daniel's Band at their nicely fitted up room, and found them all on fire for God, which cheered our hearts. The Daniel's Band arranged to have meetings in the opera house, as I was going to stay over Sunday. At five o'clock Saturday evening they began to fill the house, and by the time the meeting commenced the house was full to overflowing, and God greatly blessed the people, and several souls were saved. On Sunday the house was full all day. But Sabbath evening was the grandest and most glorious sight I ever witnessed; fully two thousand people were crowded into the hall, and fifteen or more were entranced during the evening, and God was present in mighty power. On Monday we went to New Corner, and in the evening met the Daniel's Band of that place. The house was literally packed, and there were not enough sinners in the house to fill the altar, almost everyone being on the Lord's side.

By very urgent request I next went to Tipton, Indiana. I commenced meeting on Sunday morning, April 26, 1885, at the Methodist Church, and for two weeks we held up the cross of Christ to a dying world, amidst all opposition from professing Christians and the outside world. All hell seemed arrayed against us, but I trusted in the Lord Jehovah to give us the victory. And many hundreds praise God for the meeting at Tipton.

On the second Sabbath evening, amidst the most intense excitement, when the altar was filled with seeking penitents, a Mrs. Y. went into a trance, and while in that condition, Dr. P. went to the front part of the house to see a trance for himself. She soon commenced to motion for him to get down on his knees. He fell as one dead. He yielded to the Lord; as he afterwards said, he believed it was then or never. God blessed and saved him.

I never saw such demonstrations of the Spirit and power as at this meeting. Many of the leading church members were struck down (The priests could not stand to minister because of the cloud: for the glory of the Lord had filled the house of the Lord. I Kings 8. 11.) or stood held, not able to move, under the power of God; their faces shining with the glory of God. The presence of God was so felt that the fear of the Lord fell upon all the people. (All the people greatly feared the Lord. 1 Sam. 12. 18.) In the two weeks I was here over five hundred came out on the Lord's side. May they ever be kept faithful to the end of life.

News of the wonderful work of God was spreading all over the country. The interest was so great I could not get any time to rest, day or night. Committees were sent from all parts for me to go and hold meetings in different churches. I was so exhausted from constant work I could hardly sit up. We slipped off to Indianapolis, and took boarding in a private house, hoping to rest a few days, without any one knowing where we were; but we had not been there half a day till several ministers from the city churches came to see me, and tried to persuade me to hold meetings in their churches. I told them it was impossible at that time. They then urged me to preach on Sabbath, but I had to refuse.

AT KOKOMO

After long solicitation, which had been kept up constantly for over four months, I next went to Kokomo, Indiana, and for three weeks God wonderfully blessed me and the people of that city.

My first meeting was held in the Friends' Church, which was very large. It would not hold the people. The next day we went to the court house. While there Barnum's show came to the city. The papers said there would be a race between the Woodworth meeting and the show to see who would get the biggest crowd.

Hundreds came to the city to go to the show, but when they heard of the wonderful meeting in the court house they came there. Once, while the great show was passing, I was preaching and held the crowd. We went from the court house to the skating rink, the largest building in the city. About one hundred were baptised. It was said about twenty thousand witnessed this solemn and wonderful scene. The first one baptised was a Methodist minister. About twenty church members who had not thought of being baptised were so impressed they stepped out with their best clothes on and were baptised. The crowds were so large I had to appoint three meetings that night. One was held in the court house yard and one on the street. Some ministers took charge of these meetings, and I held services in the rink. The power of God was felt for fifty miles round. Thousands of souls were brought into the light of God. The Sabbath we closed God gave us a pentecost. The Holy Ghost fell on the multitude that had crowded in the rink and around the door. The power of God had been poured out in all the meetings and rested upon the people, and "signs and wonders" followed. The Holy Ghost sat upon the bloodwashed sons and daughters of the Lord Almighty.

In two hours, five hundred converts had testified that they knew they were saved by the power of God, (Your faith should not stand in the wisdom of men, but in the power of God. (1 Cor. 2. 5.) When ye come together, every one of you hath a psalm, hath a doctrine, hath a tongue, hath a revelation. Let all things be done unto edifying. (1 Cor. 14, 26.) and happy on their way to heaven. Many fell under the power of the Holy Ghost while speaking. Many fell in all parts of the house. Old men and women wept aloud. Others shouted, and sinners cried for mercy. All classes were stricken down in the meetings; many church members and ministers of different denominations, not only in the meetings, but in the city and miles away. They had wonderful visions of hell and heaven, and many of the deep things of God. As they stood and told these visions the fear of God fell upon the people, and hundreds were convicted and brought to Christ.

One minister on his way home stopped ten miles away with some friends who had been to the meeting; while there, he fell in a trance. The news soon spread. The neighbours gathered in. One left his plough and went in. He had been fighting off conviction. As he looked at his minister lying like one dead, the Spirit of God showed him if he was not converted before he came out of the trance he would be lost forever. He fell on his knees and called upon God to save him. Others followed. The house became a mourner's bench. Soon their mourning was turned to shouts of praise. Before the minister came back from his visit to heaven, the news had been shouted around the throne: "Sinners are coming home to God." This is only one instance out of hundreds where God has started a revival far away from the meetings, by striking someone down in a trance. The great revival at Cornelius's house was all brought about by two trances, one a sinner, the other a saint, though they were many miles apart at the time. God used three visions to bring about the conversion of Saul. If I would write all the mighty works of God, I would have to write a book for each meeting.

CHAPTER 2

The Bread of Life

By Smith Wigglesworth

THE LORD HAS REVEALED TO ME A NEW ORDER concerning the Word of God. This is called the Book of Life. It is called the Spirit of Life. It is called the Son of Life. The Word of Life, the Testament of the new covenant, which has been shed in blood. There it is, the Bible. I hold it before you and it is no more than any other print without the Spirit of revelation. It is a dead letter. It is lifeless. It has no power to give regeneration. It has no power to cause new creation. It has no power to cause the new birth apart from the Spirit. It is only print. But as the Spirit of the Lord is upon us, is in us, we breathe the very nature of the life of the new creation and it becomes a quickened word. It becomes a life-giving source. It becomes the breath of the Almighty. It becomes to us a new order in the Spirit.

Interpretation of Tongues:
We shall not die, but we shall live to declare the works of the Lord. We have passed from death unto life. We are a new creation in the

Spirit. We are born of a new nature, we are quickened by a new power, we belong to a new association. Our citizenship is in heaven, from whence we look for our nature, our life, our all in all.

That is beautiful! The Spirit moving, the Spirit giving, the Spirit speaking, the Spirit making life! Can't you hear the Master say, "My Word is spirit and life?" Only by the Spirit can we understand that which is spiritual. We cannot understand it. We have to be spiritual to understand it. No man can understand the Word of God without his being quickened by the new nature. The Word of God is for the new nature. The Word of God is for the new life, to quicken mortal flesh in this order.

I read to you this morning some words from the sixth chapter of John:

> *Verily, verily I say unto you, He that believeth on me hath everlasting life. I am that bread of life. Your fathers did eat manna in the wilderness, and are dead. This is the bread which cometh down from heaven, that a man may eat thereof, and not die —John 6:47-50.*

My! I hope you have got it, for I tell you, it has changed me already. It is all new. The Word of God never is stale. It is all life. May we be so spiritually minded that it becomes life and truth to us. "I am the living bread."

Living bread! Oh, can't you feel it? Can't you eat it? Your gums will never be sore and your teeth will never ache eating this bread. The more you eat, the more you will have life. And it won't wear your body out, either. It will quicken your mortal body. This is the living bread. Feed on it. Believe it. Digest it. Let it have a real new quickening in your body.

I could sit here and listen to anybody read these verses all day and I could eat it all day. Living bread! Eternal bread!

Eternal life! Oh, the brightening of the countenance! The joy of the new nature! The hope that thrills us! The bliss that 'awaits us! Oh, the glory forever which will never decay!

Oh! For that eternal day where all are holy all are good, all are washed in Jesus' blood! But guilty sinners unrenewed come not there. There is no sickness there. This is no death there. They have never had a funeral in that land since He went. They have never known what it was to ring the death toll nor have the drum muffled. Never once has anyone died up there. No death there. No sickness. No sorrow.

Will you go there? Are you getting ready for it?

Remember this: You are created by the power of God for one purpose particularly God has no thought in creation but to bring forth through mortality a natural order that you might be quickened in the Spirit, received into glory, and worship God in a way that the angels never could. But in order that that could be, He has brought us through the flesh, quickened us by the Spirit, that we may know the love, the grace, the power, and all the prefect will of God.

He is a wonderful God — His intelligence, His superabundance in all revelation, His power to keep everything in perfect order. The sun in all its glory which is shining so majestically on the earth today is the mighty power of our glorious God, Who can make a new heaven and a new earth, wherein will dwell righteousness, where no sin will ever darken the place, where the glory of that celestial place will be wonderful.

> *I John saw the holy city, new Jerusalem, coming down from God out of heaven, prepared as a bride adorned for her husband.*

A city — figurative — not exactly figurative, luminous fact, will be, sure to be, cannot miss. A city greater than any city ever known. Millions, billions, trillions all ready for the marriage, making a great city — architecture, domes, pinnacles, cornishes, foundations — the whole city made up of saints coming to a marriage.

The glory of it! I'll be there. I shall be one of it. I do not know what part, but it will be glorious to be in it anyhow. All these billions of people will have come through tribulation, washed their robes, come through distress, brokenness of spirit, hard times, strange perplexities, weariness, and all kinds of conditions in the earth, will be quickened, made like Him, to reign with Him forever and ever.

What a thought God had when He was forming creation and making it so that we could bring forth through our loins sons and daughters in the natural, quickened by the Spirit in the supernatural, and received up to glory, and then to be made ready for a marriage! May God reveal to us our position in this Holy Ghost order that we may see how wonderful that the Lord has His mind upon us. I want you to see security, absolute security, where there will be no shaking, no trembling, no fear, absolute soundness in every way, knowing that as sure as the city is formed you are going out to the city.

Salvation is glory, new life is resurrection, new life is ascension, and this new life in God has no place for its feet anywhere between here and the glory.

The Spirit of the Lord is with us, revealing the Word, bringing to us — not eternal life, for we have that. We believe and are in this place because of that eternal life, but bringing to us a process of this eternal life, showing to us that it puts to death everything else. Eternal life came to us when we believed, but the process of eternal life can begin today, making us know that now we are sons of God.

Interpretation of Tongues:

Let thy whole heart be in a responsive place. Yield absolutely to the Spirit cry within thee. Do not be afraid of being so harmonized by the power of the Spirit that the Spirit in thee becomes so one that thou art altogether as He desires thee to be.

Do not let fear in any way come in. Let the harmonizing, spiritual life of God breathe through you that oneness, and when we get into oneness today, oh the lift, oh the difference! When our hearts are all blended in one thought, how the Spirit lifts us, how revelation can come! God is ready to take us far beyond anything we have had before.

Notice some more verses in the sixth chapter of John:

The Jews therefore strove among themselves, saying, How can this man give us his flesh to eat? Then Jesus said unto them, Verily, verily, I say unto you, Except ye eat the flesh of the Son of man, and drink his blood, ye, have no life in you. Whoso eateth my flesh, and drinketh my blood, hath eternal life; and I will raise him up at the last day. For my flesh is meat indeed, and my blood is drink indeed. He that eateth my flesh, and drinketh my blood, dwelleth in me, and I in him — John 6:52-56.

There is another word which is very lovely in the fourth chapter of the first epistle of John: "He that dwelleth in love dwelleth in God, and God in him." You cannot separate' these divine personalities. If you begin to separate the life from the nature, you will not know where you are. You will have to see that right in you the new nature is formed.

You got a glimpse of it in a very clear way in the fourth chapter of Hebrews, the twelfth verse. The Word of God — the Word, the Life, the Son, the Bread, the Spirit, in you, separating you from soulishness. The same power, the same

Spirit, separating soul and spirit, joint and marrow, right in you. The Life, the Word, the power by the Spirit quickening the mortal body. It is resurrection force. It is divine order. The stiff knee, the inactive limb, the strained position of the back, the muscles — everything in your nature resurrection power by the Word, the living Word in the body, discerning, opening, revealing hidden thoughts of the heart till the heart cannot have one thing which is absolutely contrary to God. The heart separated in thought, in life, till the whole man is brought into life divine, living in this life, moving by this power, quickened by this principle.

Oh! This is resurrection! THIS IS RESURRECTION. Is it anything else? Yes. This is that which will leave.

I do not know how far this goes, but I am told that when the spiritual life of a man is very wonderfully active, the white corpuscles in his blood are very, mightily quickened, going through the body, and after the spirit goes they cannot find them in any way. I do not know how far that goes, but to me it is a reality The Spirit of the living God flows through every vein of my body, through every tissue of my blood, and I find this life will have to go. It will have to go!

Interpretation of Tongues:

It is not by might or power, it is by my Spirit, saith the Lord. It is not the letter it is the Spirit that quickeneth. It is the resurrection which He brought into us. "I am the resurrection and the life. He that believeth in me hath resurrection life in him, resurrection power through him, and he will decrease and the resurrection will increase."

God, manifest that through us. Give us that. Oh, for this spiritual, divine appointment for us today, to see this deep, holy, inward reviving in our heart!

I must press on — I am pressing on. The only difficulty is, He is pressing in and keeps us in, holding on but laying hold. Not until in these last days have I been able to understand Paul's words to Timothy when he tells him he is to lay hold of eternal life. We cannot imagine any human man in the world laying hold of eternal life. It never could be. But a supernatural human man has power to lay hold, take hold. So it is the supernatural divine which lays hold, laying hold of eternal life.

> *Eternal life, which was with the Father, was brought to us by the Son and is of Him. As the living Father hath sent me, and I live by the Father: so he that eateth me, even he shall live by me —John 6:57*

Here is a divine principle. He had His life from the Father.

> *As I live by the Father and have life in myself by the Father, so ye shall live by me and have life from me as I take it from the Father.*

Oh, that the Lord would inspire thought and revelation in our hearts to claim this today!

This is that bread which came down from heaven: not as your fathers did eat manna, and are dead: he that eateth of this bread shall live forever — John 6:58.

It was wonderful bread that they had, it was a wonderful provision, but they ate it and they died. But God's Son became the Bread of Life, and as we eat of this bread we live forever, *forever,* FOREVER!

Interpretation of Tongues:

It is the Spirit that giveth life, for He giveth His life for us that we being dead should have eternal life. For He came to give us His own life that we henceforth should not die but live forever.

Breathe upon us,
breathe upon us,
With Thy love our hearts inspire:
Breathe upon us,
breathe upon us Lord,
baptize us now with fire.

Thank God for the breath of the Spirit, the new creation dawning. Thank God for the spiritual revelation. Fire, holy fire, burning fire, purging fire, taking the dross, everything out, making us pure gold. Fire! "He shall baptize you with the Holy Ghost, and with fire." It is a different burning to anything else. It is a burning without consuming. It is illumining. It is a different illumination to anything else. It so illumines the very nature of the man till within the inner recesses of his human nature there is a burning, holy, divine purging through till every part of dross is consumed. Carnality in all its darkness, human mind with all its blotches, inadequate to reach out, are destroyed by the fire. We shall be burned by fire till the very purity of the Christ of God shall be through and through and through till the body shall be, as it were, consumed.

It seems to me the whole of the flesh of Jesus was finished up, was consumed in the Garden, on the cross, in His tragic moments, in the twelfth chapter of John's gospel as He speaks about seed falling and as He says in the great agony with sweat upon His brow, "If it be possible."

There is a consuming of the flesh till the invisible shall become so mighty that that which is visible shall only hold its own for the invisible to come forth into the glorious blessed position of God's sonship.

These things said he in the synagogue, as he taught in Capernaum.

Many therefore of his disciples, when they had heard this, said, This is an hard saying; who can hear it? — John 6:59,60

It may be difficult for some of you clearly to understand this ministry we are giving you. Now, I tell you what to do: If you are not sitting in judgment, but allowing the Spirit to come forth to you, you will find out that that even which is a mystery will be unfolded to you and that which is a difficulty will be cleared up. These people sat in judgment without being willing to enter into the spiritual revelation of it. As I read on I want you to see how it divided the situation.

When Jesus knew in himself that his disciples murmured at it, he said unto them, Doth this offend you? — John 6:61

Jesus was a perceptive person. We too may get to the place where we rightly understand these things and can perceive the difference in the meeting, whether the people are receptive or not. I am sensitive to the fact immediately when there is anybody in the meeting who is sitting in the judgment of the meeting. Jesus felt this and said unto them:

Doth this offend you? What and if ye shall see the Son of man ascend up where he was before? It is the spirit that quickeneth; the flesh profiteth nothing: the words that I speak unto you, they are spirit, and they are life —John 6:61-63

We have been having the Word, which is life and spirit. There is not a particle of your flesh which will ever be of any advantage to you as long as you live. It has pleased God to give you a body, but only that it may be able to contain the fullness of the Godhead principles and life, and it has only been given to you that it might be so quickened with a new generation of the Spirit that you can pass through this world with salt in your life, with seasoning qualities, with light divine, with a perfect position.

He wants you walking up and down the breadth of the land, overcoming the powers of Satan, living this spiritual touch with God till your body is only used to cause you to take the spirit and the life from one quarter of the globe to the other. Quickened by Spirit. The flesh never had anything for you. The Spirit is the only property that shall help you any time. In my flesh there never has, there never will be any good thing. Only the body can be the temple of the Holy One.

Oh, to live! "If I live, I live unto Christ. If I die, I die unto Christ. Living or dying, I am the Lord's." What a wonderful word comes to us by this saintly, holy, divine person, full of holy richness! I want to say a word more about this holy man, Paul, so filled with the power of the Holy Ghost till when his flesh was torn to pieces with the rocks, the Spirit moved in his mortal life, and though his fleshly body was all the time under great privation, the Spirit moved in the life. In death oft: quickened in the Spirit. Laid out for dead: again quickened and brought to life. What a wonderful position!

"I am ready to be offered" — offered on the altar of sacrifice. By the mercy of God he lived, he moved, energized and filled with a power a million times larger than himself. In death oft, in prisons, in infirmities, in weaknesses, in all kinds of trials, but the Spirit filled his human body, and he comes to us in a climax, as it were, of soul and body mingled, with the words, "I am ready to be offered. There is the guillotine. I am ready to be offered." Already he has been on the altar of living sacrifice, and taught us how to be, but here he comes to another sacrifice, "I am ready to be offered." It is said Paul was sawn asunder. I do not know how it was, but I thank God he was ready to be offered. What a life! What a consummation. Human life consummate, eaten up by the life of another. Mortality eaten up till it has not a vestige of the human nature to say, "You shan't do that, Paul." What a consummation! What a holy invocation! What an entire separation! What a prospect of glorification!

Can it be? Yes, as surely as you are in the flesh, the same power of the quickening of the Spirit can come to you till whether in your body or out of your body you can only say, "I am not particular, just so I know":

Christ liveth in me!
Christ liveth in me!
Oh! what a salvation this,
That Christ liveth in me.

But there are some of you that believe not. For Jesus knew from the beginning who they were that believed not, and who should betray him.

And he said, Therefore said I unto you, that no man can come unto me, except it were given unto him of my Father —John 6:64,65.

It is so precisely divine in its origin that God will give this life only to those which attain unto eternal life. Do not get away from this. Every person that has eternal life, it is the purpose of the Father, it is the loyalty of God's Son, it is the assembly of the firstborn, it is the new begotten of God, it is the new creation, it is a heaven-designed race that is going to equip and get you through everything.

As sure as you are seeking now, you are in the glory. There

is a bridge of eternal security for you if you dare believe in the Word of God. There is not a drop between you and the glory. It is divine, it is eternal, it is holy, it is the life of God, and He gives it, and no man can take the life that God gives to you from you. Wonderful! It is almightiness. Its production is absolutely unique. It is so essential, in the first place; it is so to be productive, in the next place; it is so to be changed, in the third place; it is so to be seated, in the fourth place. It is God's nature which cannot rest in the earth. It is His nature from heaven. It is a divine nature. It is an eternal power. It is an eternal life. It belongs to heaven. It must go back from whence it came.

I hope no person will say, "Wigglesworth is preaching eternal security." I am not. I have a thousand times better things in my mind than that. My preaching is this: I know I have that which shall not be taken away from me. "Mary hath chosen that good part, which shall not be taken away from her."

I am dwelling upon the sovereignty, the mercy, and the boundless love of God. I am dwelling upon the wonderful power of God's order. The heavens, the earth, and under the earth is submissive to the Most High God. All demon power has to give place to the royal kinship of God's eternal throne. Every knee shall bow every devil shall be submitted, and God will bring us some day right in the fullness of the blaze of eternal bliss, and the brightness of His presence will cast every unclean spirit and every power of devils into the pit forever and ever and ever.

Interpretation of Tongues:

Why faint, then, at tribulation when these light afflictions, which are only for a moment, are working out for us an eternal, glorious weight of glory. For we see this: That God, in His great plan of preparing, has delivered us from the corruption of the world and transformed us and made us able to come into the image of the Most Holy One. We are made free from the law of sin and death because the life of Christ has been manifest in our mortal body. Therefore, we live — and yet we live not but another life, another power and eternal force, a resurrection glory.

O Jesus! If our fellowship here be so sweet, if the touches of the eternal glory move our inspiration, what must it be to be there!

> *From that time many of his disciples went back, and walked no more with him. Then said Jesus unto the twelve, Will ye also go away? Then Simon Peter answered him, Lord to whom shall we go? thou hast the words of eternal life — John 6:66-68*

Where will you go? If you leave the Master, where will you go? Where can we go? If we need a touch in our bodies, where can we go? If we want life, where can we go? Is there anywhere? This world is a big world, but tell me if you can get it.

Could you get it if you soared the heights of the Alps of Switzerland and looked over those glassy mountains where the sun is shining? As I peeped over one of those mountains one morning I saw eleven glaciers and three lakes, like diamonds before me in the glittering sun. I wept and I wept, but I did not get consolation. Then I dropped on my knees and looked to God — then I got consolation.

Where shall we go? There are all the grandeurs and the glories of earth to be seen, but they do not satisfy me. They all belong to time. They will all fold up like a garment that is laid aside. They will all melt with fervent heat.

Where shall we go? "Thou only hast the words of eternal life." Jesus, You fed us with bread from heaven. Jesus, give us Your life. Oh, breathe it into us! Then we will eat and drink and breathe and think in God till our own nature is eaten up with the life divine, where we are perpetually in the sweetness of His divine will, in the glory — already in! Praise Him!

You can always be holy. You can always be pure. It is the mind of the Spirit that is making you know holiness, righteousness, Rapture.

Questions and Answers

Q: *Is any part of the mission of the Holy Ghost to purify and cleanse from sin?*

A: We have nowhere specified in the Scriptures that the Holy Ghost is a cleanser, but there is a great power in the Spirit. Rudiments of evil, sins, covetousness, adultery, fornication, and a thousand other things that may have been in the body, when the Spirit got revelation through that body, He would bring Christ in evidence so that the Word of God would come true as in Romans 8:10: "And if Christ be in you, the body is dead because of sin; but the Spirit is life because of righteousness."

Wherever Jesus is manifested in the body, sin is dethroned in that body. Jesus is the dethroner of sin and the cleanser by His blood and the purifier of the mind, and sets the whole body in perfect contract with heaven, as He is made manifest in the mortal body.

The moment sin is dethroned, the moment every carnal power is removed, the next thing that happens in the body, he wants to do justly, he wants to live righteously. And the moment righteousness takes place in the body, then the Holy Spirit has greater illumination to that soul, and he leaps and leaps and goes on and sees new things in Christ than he saw before.

The sanctification of the Spirit, as referred to in 1 Peter 1:2, keeps the baptized believer humble, keeps him broken, keeps him separate, keeps him realizing the spirit of revelation of the powers of demon power. When the evil power as an angel of light comes and says, "You are wonderful! You are mighty! There is no one like you!" then the Holy Spirit can so lay hold of you and make you broken, empty, helpless, weakened before God — and that is the sanctification of the Spirit. God help us to see that we need the sanctification of the Spirit in the day of triumph.

Q: *There is a teaching that the emblems we partake of at the Communion time are the actual flesh and blood of Jesus, our Lord. Is that right?*

A: Jesus said it was His blood. He said it was His body and that they had to eat of it. If they had actually eaten Him around that table, He would have been incomplete as a sacrifice. But He was as whole after they had that meal as He was before.

The people who teach this are deluded, and it is the delusion of the devil. The Romans have been deluded all through the years.

It never is and never will be the body and the blood of Jesus. It is an emblem and leads you to the real presence of the Lord.

Q: *Is the husband that is not saved a hindrance to the wife receiving her healing?*

A: Corinthians has a big place for the husband and wife. Every unsaved husband can be sanctified by the sanctification of the wife, and vice versa. If the husband or the wife is not saved, or if they are both not saved and are seeking healing, if any ministering saint of God would go, God would minister life and healing for revelation to those people and bring them to a knowledge of the truth by a manifestation. God worked in Australia and in New

Zealand, bringing family after family into the knowledge of the truth because one person was healed in the family — a manifestation of the power of God. I believe that nothing in the home will interfere with divine healing excepting unbelief.

Q: *Please explain the Scripture that says, "If you believe on the name of Jesus, you and your house will be saved."*
A: A lot of people are terribly troubled about their families. I wish you would get to the place of faith. God's Word says it, you believe it, and they will be saved. Why should you take anything else? My wife and I agreed together to believe this scripture, and He was faithful Who promised and saved our children.

Q: *Will you explain what place testimony should have in the service and what place the Word should have? Is it in the proper order that testimony should crowd out the preaching of the Word?*
A: If you do not allow testimony in your meetings, you will impoverish the church. The more you testify, the more sanguine you are in your salvation. Every time you testify, the spring of prophecy will come forth and make you know your glorious originality is perfect in God. It would help any meeting to have half an hour's testimony at the commencement, if you felt the spirit of testimony coming. Then you have a right to let the Word follow that, because it ought to follow that. There must be order on the line of the prophecy. If there is a great unction on the people to testify, and you see there is prophecy coming through them, patiently say, "Now beloved, it is time for the ministry of the Word. Let us see how many testimonies we can have in the next five minutes."

People want love. They want grace, and they want it administered in love.

Q: *Are the results mentioned in Mark 16:16-18 to be only to those who are baptized with the Holy Spirit?*

A: Thousands of people who have never received the baptism of the Holy Ghost are very specially led and blessed in healing the sick. The finest people that ever I did know have never come into the same experience as I am in today regarding the baptism of the Holy Spirit, are mightily used with all kinds of sicknesses wonderfully. But they did not have that which is in the sixteenth chapter of Mark. Only baptized believers speak in tongues. "If you believe, you shall lay hands on the sick, and if you believe, you shall speak in new tongues" — meaning to say, after the Holy Ghost is come, you are in the place of command. You can command. How do I know it? Because Paul, in 2 Timothy is very clear when he says, "Stir up the gift."

What was the trouble with Timothy? He was downcast. He was a young man, called out by Paul, had been amongst the presbytery, and because of his youth he had been somewhat put to one side, and he was grieved. Paul found him in a distressed place, so Paul stirred him up.

Every one of you, if you have faith, can stir up the gift within you. The Holy Ghost can be so manifest in you that you can speak. It may not be in gift, but speak in utterances by tongues. And I believe everybody baptized in the Holy Ghost has a right to allow the Spirit to have perfect control and speak every day, morning, noon, and night in this order.

Do not put out your hand to stop anybody that is doing good, but bring them in the baptism of much good.

CHAPTER 3

Modes of Healing
By John G Lake

THERE ARE FOUR MODES OF HEALING, and more than that, but four principle modes taught in the Word of God. The first is the direct prayer of faith of those, who just like the leper, come to Jesus and say, "Lord, if thou wilt, thou canst make me clean." Jesus answered the leper, "I will; be thou clean" (Matthew 8:2–3; Mark 1:40–41; Luke 5:12–13). And His "I will" has rung down through the ages, for He healed all who came to Him. (See, for example, Matthew 4:24, 8:16; Luke 6:19.) He never turned one of them away. And in healing all that came to Him, He demonstrated forever what the will of God concerning sickness was.

"But, brother," you say, "are all the people healed whom you pray for?" No, they are not, and it is my sorrow; for I believe that if I was in the place before God where old Peter was and Paul was, bless God, all the people would be healed. And it is the purpose of my soul to let God take my soul into that place of real communion and consciousness of the power of God, through Jesus Christ, where all the people—not just some of the people—are healed.

However, beloved, I want to say that God made me too much of a man to try to dodge the issue and throw the responsibility off on God. My! How the church has worked at this acrobatic trick of throwing the responsibility over on God.

> *These signs shall follow them that believe:...they shall lay hands on the sick, and they shall recover. (Mark 16:17–18)*

Now, here is a sick man, and here comes the minister. As he gets close to him, the minister sees he is pretty bad. He is in trouble. He says to himself, "If I pray for him and he is not healed, the people will think I have not much faith in God." So he does the acrobatic trick and says, "It may not be the will of God that you should be healed." Do you see it?

How many did Jesus heal? All who came to Him; and in healing them all, He gave to mankind forever the finality concerning the will of God about healing the sick.

There is no further point to go in demonstration than Jesus went on the subject of the will of God. If He had ever turned one poor fellow away and said, "No, it is not God's will to heal you," then there could be a question mark set up; but having healed them all, He left the will of God concerning sickness forever settled and indelibly stamped forever on the human mind.

I am glad we know that kind of a Christ. An awful lot of people have been sent down the broad way through that old lie about the will of God and sickness.

"Well, brother," you say, "how are you going to get the people to heaven, if they are all healed? Why, they will live forever." Well, bless God, I am going one step further. However, we have not reached the place of faith yet where it is applicable in our lives. We are still discussing healing for the body.

Jesus said,

> *Your fathers did eat manna in the wilderness and are dead. This is the bread which cometh down from heaven, that a man may eat thereof, and not die. I am the living bread which came down from heaven: if any man eat of this bread, he shall live forever....And whosoever liveth and believeth in me shall never die. Believest thou this?*
> *—John 6:49–51, 11:26*

And many of His disciples turned away and walked no more with Him. (See John 6:66.) They said, "This is an hard saying; who can hear [receive] it?" (verse 60).

The faith of the church has never reached up to the place where we could dare to claim it. But beloved, I praise God that an ever-increasing number of men and women are rising up every day, who will enjoy stepping over the boundary into that hundredfold consecration, where they will consecrate once and forever their bodies and their souls and their spirits to God. Blessed be His name.

The consecration of the body to God is just as sacred as the consecration of the soul. No man can understand what the Christian life ought to be, what Jesus intended it to be, until the person sees the consecration that He made of Himself to the will of God. It is a pattern consecration for every other Christian. He was the first Christian, blessed be God. He consecrated His spirit to God, His soul to God, His body to God. Each was equally precious in the sight of God. Think of it!

Suppose that just once in His lifetime, when in trouble concerning the things of the Spirit, He had gone to the devil for help. Would He have been the spotless Lamb of God? Never! He would have been blemished. Suppose that in His mental distress, He had turned to the world for help and accepted the spirit of the world as His comforter. He would have been blemished in His soul life. He would not have been the spotless Lamb of God. Suppose one morning you would see the Lord Jesus sneaking around the back door into a drugstore to get ten cents' worth of pills for His body. Can you imagine such a thing? It is too horrible to imagine. If He had, He would never have been the spotless Lamb of God. He would have been blemished in His faith for His body before His Father.

But because the Christ demonstrated His power to trust God for His spirit, for His soul, and for His body, He became the author of eternal salvation and was able to present Himself to God a spotless conqueror and unblemished sacrifice.

And the hundredfold Christian, who received through the Holy Ghost the power of God and the dominion of the spirit, will present himself to God in the same manner— body and soul and spirit—unto God, a reasonable sacrifice and service (see Romans 12:1.) Blessed be His precious name.

Know ye not that your body is the temple of the Holy Ghost which is in you? –1 Corinthians 6:19

Shall I take this temple that I endeavor, by the grace of God, to lend to God for the purpose that He may dwell in my life by the Spirit, and fill it up with cocaine or digitalis or some of the other thousand and one damnable things that destroy human life and produce abnormal conditions in the system? Never, if I am a hundredfold child of God!

Here again is the ministerial acrobat with the gifts of the Holy Ghost.

> *To one is given by the Spirit the word of wisdom; to another the word of knowledge by the same Spirit; to another faith by the same Spirit; to another the gifts of healing by the same Spirit; to another the working of miracles, to another prophecy; to another discerning of spirits; to another divers kinds of tongues; to another the interpretation of tongues. —1 Corinthians 12:8–10*

Paul said correctly that not all have these various gifts. That is perfectly correct. But beloved, the subject of gifts has nothing whatever to do with the principle of faith in God. The gifts are entirely extraordinary. The normal life of a real Christian with faith in God commands the power of God for his own need through faith. Have you ever noticed that the anointing with oil and the prayer of faith that saves the sick (see James 5:14–15) have nothing to do with the gifts of healing? It is an entirely different operation of healing. The elder or the priest comes in the name of Jesus. He anoints the man with oil and prays the prayer of faith. The prayer that expresses my faith in God that He will raise this man up is the prayer of faith. It is not the gift of healing at all, but simply the prayer of faith.

How far is it applicable? Jesus said,

> *If two of you shall agree on earth as touching anything that they shall ask, it shall be done for them of my Father which is in heaven. —Matthew 18:19*

The first healing I ever knew was the healing of a Roman Catholic girl who had formerly worked for my wife. Seven members in her family had died of consumption between the ages of eighteen and twenty-one. She was the last of the family. At the age of twenty, the disease appeared in her likewise. She was engaged to be married to a splendid fellow, but day by day she withered away, just as the others had done.

In those days I knew nothing about healing through God. A friend came to her and said, "Mary, let us observe a novena." That is nine days of prayer. These two women, without any help from anyone, and who knew little or nothing of the Word of God, believing in the Christ as their Savior, began to pray throughout the nine days that God by His mighty power would raise the woman up. Her friend said, "When the Lord heals you, get up and come to my house." So on the ninth morning, when the time was complete and Mary did not appear at the friend's house, she got troubled and started down to see about it; and on the road, she met her coming. God had met the faith of two poor, simple women who had no teaching whatever on the subject of healing.

Among all the classes of people who come to our healing rooms, we find that Roman Catholics receive healing more readily than any other particular class of church people. You ask me why. They are educated to have faith in God. They are not educated to doubt Him. A great deal of modern preaching is an education in doubt concerning God. If you cannot explain the thing and you cannot demonstrate it, over you go, turn a somersault, and tell them it means something else.

A friend of mine in the city, who is a ministerial brother, used to be my pastor in the Methodist church when I was a young man. He was assistant pastor. Now he is one of the great ecclesiastical lights. I remember a sermon of his. He was explaining the fall of the walls of Jericho. Paul wrote:

"By faith the walls of Jericho fell down, after they were compassed about seven days" (Hebrews 11:30). "By faith," by the united faith of the people who dared to believe God, the very walls crumbled and came down. Their instructions were to encircle the city seven days and on the seventh day to go around it seven times; and when the final march was completed, the priests, with their trumpets and their rams' horns, were to sound a blast of triumph to God, and the people were to give the shout of faith. When they had sounded, the walls came down, by faith.

My friend very wisely said, "Every structure has a key note, and if you just find and sound the key note of the structure, down it will come. The wise priests sounded the key note and down the walls of Jericho came." That was his vision; Paul had a different one. He said, "By faith the walls of Jericho fell down, after they were compassed about seven days."

Faith is not always characterized by beautiful phrases or sweet prayers. I had a minister in my work in South Africa, a very strong, vigorous man. He had a military training background; he was an officer in the army during the Boer war. His name was W. I had another minister who was a nice, sweet, gentle, tender man named J. He had none of the strong qualities that W. possessed, but he loved God and had faith in Him.

One evening a Church of England minister sent in a call about his wife, who was dying of a cancer. The doctors could do nothing more, and now they wanted to trust God. That is where a lot of people get to. May God almighty have mercy on you. They are what we call "last resorters." We have an expression among ourselves: "Is he a last resorter?"

I reasoned that it would never do to send Brother W. down to that house, because he was such a strenuous man. He was likely to shock them. I said, "I will send Brother J.

because he is one of those nice, polished men." So he went down and prayed for quite a long time. The rector knelt reverently at the foot of the bed and prayed with him, but there was no evidence of a real healing. After a while the telephone rang, and Brother J. was on the line. He said, "Brother Lake, I wish you would send W. down here; I cannot get the victory, and I need help."

I said, "Surely, I will." So I told Brother W. to go down and help him. He said, "All right, I will go," and away he started. When he arrived, he said, "What is the trouble, Brother J.?"

He said, "I do not know."

W. said, "Let us pray again." As he prayed, he said, "You damnable cancer, get to hell and out of here, in the name of Jesus Christ." The Spirit of God flamed in him, and the power of God fell on the woman. The cancer withered, and the woman was healed. After a while the telephone rang again. Brother J. said, "It is all right, Brother; she is healed, but the rector has not recovered from the effect of Brother W.'s prayer yet."

Bless God! There is something better than polished phrases. It is the faith of God that permits a soul to break through the darkness and the doubt that the devil and the world and the unbelieving church has heaped upon the souls of men.

It takes the power of God and the faith of God to break the bands that bind men's souls and get them through into the daylight of God. That is where healing, real healing, is found. I wish I could take a whole lot of you sick folks and get you broke through into the presence of God. You would not have to come to the healing rooms day after day if you did.

I have a conviction that there are mighty few Christian ministers who can tell you what divine healing is. In the world at large, I know there is a great deal of confusion. There is natural healing, medical healing, psychological healing, and there is divine healing. I am quoting my brother Beatty now. We recognize them all, but I want to tell you, beloved, the real Christian, the hundredfold Christian, the person who gives himself to God and receives the power of God, is not fooling around with medical healing, and not psychological healing either. They are good enough in their place, but God has given a better way and a higher way. There is as much difference between spiritual and psychological healing as there is between natural or medical and psychological healing. It is a higher plane and the higher life by a higher power, the power of God through the Holy Spirit.

Jesus demonstrated that to us so beautifully. He was walking down the road, and a poor woman, who had an issue of blood for twelve years, said within herself, "If I may but touch his garment, I shall be whole" (Matthew 9:21). You say that was faith. She could have had faith in a bread pill, because the doctors tell you if you have not faith in them, their drugs will do no good. You see, the virtue is not located in the remedy. It is in what you think of the doctor and your confidence in him. Every good doctor knows that fact.

It was not her faith in the sense we usually talk about faith. It was the virtue that was in Him. "If I could just touch the hem of His garment, I would be healed." How did she know it? Because she saw that those upon whom He laid His hands received virtue and were made whole. The virtue that was in Him flowed out and healed them. So she stole up in the crowd and touched the hem of His garment; and, bless God, His very clothing was filled with the virtue of God, and it flowed from the garment to the woman, and she felt in her body that she was made whole, and Jesus felt it too.

Peter said, "Master, don't You see the multitude that is

thronging You, and yet You say, 'Somebody touched me'?"

"Yes, but I perceive that virtue hath gone out of me." Hers was a different touch. It was the touch that received the life of the Christ into her own being. (See Luke 8:43-48.)

Divine healing is life, the life of God. Healing is transmitted into your being, whether it comes from heaven upon your own soul or is transmitted through a man of faith. It does not make any difference. It is the touch of the living Christ.

But you say, "Jesus was Jesus. Other men did not have that virtue."

Do you remember Paul, when they brought handkerchiefs and aprons in order that they might touch his body? (See Acts 19:12.) Then they were taken to the sick, and the sick were healed. Here is dear old Paul. A mother comes to him. "Oh, Paul, I have a sick boy at my house. He is dying of epilepsy, or typhoid fever, or cancer. Paul, here is my apron. Take it so that the Spirit of God will flow into it from your being." Then she takes the apron home with her and puts it on the boy, and the power of God that was in the apron flows out of it into the boy, and the boy is healed. That is divine healing.

So it is with every man who is really baptized in the Holy Ghost. Last Wednesday night, as our service was about to commence, I laid my Bible on the table. A man came in and took up the Bible and dropped it as though it was hot.

Then a woman sitting nearby reached out and took it up, and the power of God came upon her and she commenced to shake. They said, "Isn't that strange!" Not at all. That is the Bible over which Brother Westwood and Brother Fogwill and I kneel in the healing rooms and ask God to open its blessed pages, that we may understand the Spirit of the Word of God and receive the power of God that makes these people well. I believe the very paper becomes saturated with the power of God.

Both animate and inanimate objects can become filled with the Spirit of God. Even the bones of those who have trusted in the living God have retained their virtue. The old prophet [Elisha] had been in his grave many a day, when one day in their haste to bury a man, they opened the same grave in which the prophet's bones lay. But when the dead man touched the bones of that Holy Ghost-filled man, he became a living man and rose up well. (See 2 Kings 13:21.)

Oh, the most vital thing in all the universe is the Holy Spirit. It is more real than electricity, more powerful than gravity. It is more subtle than the ether in the air. It contains more energy than any natural power. It is the vitality of the living God, the fire of His soul, the very substance of His being. Bless God! Open your nature to God. Receive the Christ into your heart. Confess your sins and acknowledge the Lord Jesus Christ as your Savior. Receive Him as your Savior and Healer now, and God will bless you.

CHAPTER 4

Questions and Answers on Divine Healing
By Maria Woodworth-Etter

Q. *What is divine healing?*
A. Divine healing is the act of God's grace, by the direct power of the Holy Spirit, by which the physical body is delivered from sickness and disease and restored to soundness and health.

Q. *Have we any promise in the Bible that Divine healing was ever intended to be an attainable blessing to the people of God?*
A. Yes. There are many such promises. We find it given to the people of Israel in a special covenant promise. "If thou wilt diligently hearken to the voice of the Lord thy God, and wilt do that which is right in His sight, and wilt give ear to His commandments, and keep all His statutes, I will put none of these diseases upon thee, which I have brought upon the Egyptians; for I am the Lord that healeth thee." Ex. 15. 26. "And ye shall serve the Lord your God, and He shall bless thy bread and thy water; and I will take sickness

away from the midst of thee." Ex. 23. 25.

Q. *Does the Bible prove that any of the people of God ever enjoyed this blessing?*
A. Yes. We read that even before this covenant blessing was promised the physical condition of the people was perfect, which indicates plainly that God had a special interest in their health. See Ps. 105. 37. There were at least two and one-half million people in the Exodus from Egypt, "and there was not one feeble person among their tribes." Moses enjoyed this blessing in a special manner. Deut. 34. 7. So also did Caleb in an unusual experience of preservation and health to an old age. Josh. 14. 10, 11. David personally knew of the benefits and blessings of healing. Ps. 6. 2; 30. 2; 103. 1-4. Whenever Israel lived up to the covenant conditions; they all had the benefits of healing and health. Ps. 107. 20; 2 Chron. 30. 20. Hezekiah had a personal experience of the same. 2 Kings 20. 1-5.

Q. *Was this blessing ever promised to anyone else than the Jews?*
A. Yes. It is given in prophecy as a redemption blessing, which, together with all other gospel blessings through Christ, is offered to both Jew and Gentile. Gal. 3. 27-29.

Q. *What does prophesy say about divine healing?*
A. There is more said about it in prophecy than we have time at present to read, but I will just quote a few verses, and the rest can be read at your leisure. " Then the eyes of the blind shall be opened, and the ears of the deaf shall be unstopped. Then shall the lame leap as an hart, and the tongue of the dumb sing." Isa. 35. 5, 6. This very prophecy is referred to by Jesus Himself in Matt. 11. 5, 6, where it was daily being fulfilled, "The blind receive their sight, and the lame walk, the lepers are cleansed, and the deaf hear, the dead are raised

up, and the poor have the gospel preached to them." Another very plain prophecy is found in Isa. 53. 4 "Surely He hath borne our grief's, and carried our sorrows." The fulfilment of this wonderful voice of inspiration is found in Matt. 8. 17 - "Himself took our infirmities and bore our sicknesses." It is admitted by all reliable translators and the most eminent Hebrew scholars, such as Barnes, Magee, Young and Leeser, that Isa. 53. 4 in its literal rendering corresponds exactly with Matt. 8. 17. We see, therefore, that the latter is a direct reference to the former. Then the beautiful prophecy of salvation and healing is found in the following verse, viz.: Isaiah 53. 5- "But He was wounded for our transgressions, He was bruised for our iniquities; the chastisement of our peace was upon Him; and with His stripes we are healed." These prophecies all point to the Redemption work of Jesus, which finds its centre in the Cross. The apostle Peter refers to this verse just quoted in the following language: "Who His own self bare our sins in His own body on the tree, that we, being dead to sins, should live unto righteousness: by whose stripes ye were healed." 1 Pet. 2. 24. The following references will enable you to see that more is said in prophecy about healing: Isaiah 42. 7; Isaiah 61. 1. Fulfilled in Luke 4. 18-21. Prophecy in Mal. 4. 2. Fulfilled in Matt. 4. 16; Luke 1. 78, 79. These are all fulfilled in redemption.

Q. *Do you believe that the Bible teaches divine healing as a redemption blessing?*

A. Yes. Do you not see how plain this is made in the prophecies just quoted and in their fulfilment? Jesus worked in every respect, in His life, ministry, death and resurrection, just according to the redemption plan. His words and deeds are the divine expression of this redemption plan, and we can clearly see that healing for the body is placed upon equality with healing for the soul. Both are obtained upon the same grounds, obedience and faith.

Q. *Can a person possess salvation without healing?*
A. Yes, he may. While both are obtained by faith, yet they may not both be obtained by the same act of faith. Jesus will be to us just what our faith takes Him for.

Q. *Did Jesus heal everybody?*
A. Yes; all who came to Him in faith. Read Matt. 4. 23, 24 and Matt. 12. 15.

Q. *But they did not seem to have faith, did they?*
A. Yes. If you read the references just mentioned, you will notice the people "came to Him" for healing, and "followed Him." At Nazareth, His own town, where He had been brought up, He could do no great work among them, because of their unbelief. At Capernaum, where some of the most remarkable healings were wrought, the people were a believing people. Out of nineteen of the most prominent individual cases of healing in the ministry of Christ and the apostles, there are twelve of these where their faith is spoken of. The rest are mentioned sufficiently plainly to show that faith brought the healing in every case.

Q. *Did not Jesus heal arbitrarily, for the sole purpose of establishing His divinity?*
A. No. He healed according to the law of redemption, and because of His great compassion to suffering humanity. Matt. 14.14.

Q. *Did not healing cease when Jesus finished His earthly ministry?*
A. No. It was more wonderfully manifested in the ministry of the apostles after the day of Pentecost. Acts 5. 12,16; 3. 1-

16; 14. 8-10; 9. 17, 18; 8. 6-8; 19. 11, 12; 14. 19, 20; 9. 33-35; 9. 36-42; 20. 8-12; 28. 3-6, 8. This proves clearly that divine healing is a redemption blessing for the entire Holy Spirit dispensation.

Q. *But we are taught that it was only for the beginning of the gospel dispensation. How about that?*
A. The Bible does not teach any such doctrine.

Q. *But it does teach that "when that which is perfect is come, then that which is in part shall be done away." 1 Cor. 13. 10. How about this?*
A. This scripture has no reference to divine healing or any of the redemption blessings, that they shall be done away in this dispensation. If there ever has been a time in this dispensation when it could have been said with reference to the full possession and manifestation of the gospel blessings, that "that which is perfect is come," it was when the Holy Spirit came at Pentecost; but we see after this mighty works of salvation and healing, and they were in no sense "done away" with, but were greatly increased. So you see the "done away" argument has no scriptural basis whatever. As long as the dispensation of grace shall last, so long shall the benefits of grace be extended to "whomsoever will."

Q. *Well, then, when was divine healing done away?*
A. In the design of God it was never done away.

Q. *Do you mean to say that it was perpetuated in the primitive church?*
A. Certainly it was. History shows that for several centuries there was no other means of healing practiced in the church.

Q. *But what after that?*
A. Just what crowded out all other gospel truths - the superstitions and unbelief of the apostasy. But, thank God,

the darkness is past and the Sun of Righteousness with healing in His wings is shining salvation and health to all who will forsake all their old doctrines, creeds and superstitions, and get back upon the old apostolic foundation, the Word of God.

Q. *But how may I know that it is still God's will to heal?*
A. Just as you may know that it is His will to save by His Word. His Word is His will.

Q. *But it may be His will not to heal me.*
A. You must go outside of God's Word to find standing ground for such a conclusion; for there is nothing inside of the Bible about healing but what corresponds with our blessed text: "Himself took our infirmities and bare our sicknesses." Most people who argue that it might not be God's will to heal them are at the same time taking medicine and employing every possible human agency to get well. Why be so inconsistent? Why fight against God's will. If it is His will for you not to get well, then die. Stop fighting against God.

Q. *But does not sickness come from God as a blessing?*
A. No. It never comes from God only in a permissive sense, the same as a temptation comes to us; and sickness is never a blessing to us only as any other temptation or trial may be considered a blessing. The blessing is in the deliverance and healing. Every person who has ever experienced the healing touch of God knows what a blessing to the soul comes with it. Sickness is an abnormal condition of the body and cannot be a blessing from God.

Q. *If it does not come from God, then where does it come from?*
A. It comes from the Devil and was always dealt with by

Jesus in His earthly ministry as a work of the Devil. The Word of God plainly teaches us that the Devil is the author of disease. Read John 2. 7; Luke 13. 16; Acts 10. 38.

Q. *But are there not some other scriptures that teach us that sickness comes from God?*
A. Only in a permissive sense.

Q. *Does the Bible teach us that God intends to be the Healer of His people without the use of medicine?*
A. Yes. It nowhere commands the use of medicine with prayer and faith.

Q. *But how about Hezekiah's figs, the blind man's clay, and Timothy's wine?*
A. It is true Isaiah told Hezekiah to take a lump of figs, but this has nothing to do with the New Testament means of healing. Also it is very evident that the figs did not heal him; but God said, "I will heal thee." Jesus did not use the clay on the eyes of the blind man for any curative power, for He commanded the man at once to go and wash it off. No one has heard of blindness from birth being healed by the use of clay as a medicine since then, or ever before. It is evident that the spittle and clay were used by Jesus as a requirement of submission and obedience from the blind man. The thought must have been repulsive and humiliating to him as the clay was applied to his eyes, but, like Naaman, he submitted and obeyed and received the blessing unspeakable, of healing. Wine was recommended to Timothy as an article of diet, and would not be objectionable to day, in its proper use, under similar circumstances.

Q. *Are not medicines recognised in the Word of God?*
A. Yes. Let us read how it recognises them. "Thou hast no

healing medicines." Jer. 30. 13. "In vain shalt thou use many medicines." Jer. 46. 11. "A merry heart doeth good (like) medicine" (there is no Hebrew for the word "like," showing that the merry heart is the medicine). Prov. 17. 22. "And the fruit thereof shall be for meat, and the leaf thereof for medicine." Ezek. 47. 12. This latter reference is prophetical of the tree of life and divine healing. See Rev. 22. 2. Thus we see the Word of God places no intrinsic value upon medicine.

Q. *Is not the ministry of physicians for the body designed of God, the same as the ministry of the gospel for the soul?*

A. No. The greater portion of the physicians of the land are ungodly people, many of them professed infidels, and were never designed of God to administer drugs and poisons to anyone; much less to the people of God, whose bodies are the sacred temples of the Holy Spirit. The true ministers of the gospel are the ministers for soul and body. "And they departed, and went through the towns, preaching the gospel, and healing everywhere." Luke 9. 6. "And they went forth, and preached everywhere, the Lord working with them, and confirming the word with signs following." Mark 16. 20.

Q. *But is not the ministry of physicians recognised in the Bible?*

A. Yes. Let us read how it recognises them. "But ye are forgers of lies, ye are all physicians of no value." Job. 13. 4. " And Asa in the thirty and ninth year of his reign was diseased in his feet, until his disease was exceeding great; yet in his disease he sought not to the Lord, but to the physicians." 2 Chron. 16. 12. "And had suffered many things of many physicians, and had spent all that she had, and was nothing bettered, but rather grew worse." Mark 5. 26. These scriptures show that the Bible gives no very favourable recognition of physicians.

Q. *Was not anointing with oil the mode of doctoring in Bible times?*
A. No. While some kinds of oil may have some medical value for some kinds of diseases, it was not at all designed for any such use in connection with the prayer of faith in healing the sick. If anointing was the mode of doctoring, the church would have had no need of instruction in this respect; for it would have been a common practice everywhere by the doctors, and had this been the mind of the apostle, then he would have assigned the work of anointing to the doctors, "Elders are not Masseurs."

CHAPTER 5

Second Corinthians 3

By Smith Wigglesworth

ALL THOUGHTS OF HOLINESS ARE GOD'S. All manner of loving kindness and tender mercies are His. All weaknesses are made for us that we might be in that place of absolute helplessness, for when we are weak, then we are strong. All divine acquaintance with Him today will put us in the place where we may be the broken, empty vessel, ready for Christ's use.

> *Whom have I in heaven beside Thee? And there is none on earth but Thee.*

Oh! That is a wonderful place, where all your springs are in Him, all your desires are after Him, and you long only for Him.

Get ready that you may be touched by His inward earnestness this morning, that you may see the power of possibility in an impossible place, till you may see that God can change you, till you will change other things, till you may see today that your song will keep on the wing.

Are you ready? What for? That God shall be all in all and you will lose your identity in the perfection of His glorified purity. You will be lost to everything else except Him.

Are you ready? What for? That you may come to the banquet house with a great faith, nothing stopping you, pressing into, laying hold of, believing all things, and you will have a time of great refreshing as you come expressing yourself to God.

We must not stop this holy pursuit. We must remember that whatever shall happen in these days is happening for our future benefit. If it deals with the flesh, with the carnal senses at all, and with the human spirit, it is that God has to have a right-of-way till we will live in the Spirit.

In 2 Corinthians the third chapter we have a very blessed word. If you get this truth into your heart, you will not be moved any more by anything. This is just the difference between the human and the divine. If human is there, prominent, then divine vision will be dimmed. *When the divine has the full control, then all earthly cares and anxieties pass away. If we live in the Spirit, we are over all human animal nature. If we reach the climax that God's Son said we had to come into, we shall always be in the place of peace.*

> *If ye abide in me and my words abide in you, ye shall ask what ye will and it shall be done unto you" —John 15:7*

Jesus was a manifestation of power to dethrone every evil thing, and He dealt always with the flesh. It was necessary for Him to say to Peter, "Get thee behind me, Satan, for thou savourest the things that be of man and not of God." Everything that interferes with your plan of putting to death the old man is surely the old man that is comforting you.

There is a rest of faith if we have entered into it, ceased from our own works, ceased from our own struggling, ceased from making our own plans. It is a rest in faith, a place where you can smile in the face of any eruption. No matter what came, you would be in the place of real rest. It is in the position of this word in the third chapter of 2 Corinthians.

Epistles of Christ

Do we begin again to commend ourselves? or need we, as some others, epistles of commendation to you, or letters of commendation from you? You are our epistle written in our hearts, known and read of all men; forasmuch as ye are manifestly declared to be the epistle of Christ ministered by us, written not with ink, but with the Spirit of the living God – 2 Corinthians 3:1-3

Here we have a very remarkable word which the Spirit wants to enlarge on us. It is true that we must be the epistle of Christ. The epistle of Christ is a living power in the mortal flesh, quickening, dividing asunder everything which is not of the Spirit, till you realize that now you live in a new order. It is the Spirit that has manifested Himself in your mortal body. The Word has become life. It has quickened you all through, and you are not in any way subject to anything around you. You are above everything. You reign above everything.

You are evidently sent forth this morning by the Word of God as the epistles of Christ, meaning to say that all human ideals, plans and wishes for the future are past. For you to live is Christ. For you to live is to be His epistle, emblematic, divinely sustained by another power greater than you. You do not seek your own any more. You are living in a place where God is on the throne, superintending your human life,

God changing everything and making you understand this wonderful truth.

I believe it would be good to read just a little word in the next chapter:

> *For God, who commanded the light to shine out of darkness, hath shined in our hearts, to give the light of the knowledge of the glory of God in the face of Jesus Christ. But we have this treasure in earthen vessels, that the excellency of the power may be of God, and not of us. −2 Cor 4:6-7*

The excellency of the power of the life of Christ in the mortal body, subduing it in every way till the Spirit is full of life and vitality in the body, that Christ, that God, and the Holy Ghost may be illuminating the whole body. The body is there just as the temple, that all the glory should roll back to God. Not seeking your own, not seeking your place, but all your body giving place to the glorifying of the Christ. Set free, loosed, created by and made likened unto Him in this glorious order.

Live Not Under the Law

If you go at any time into law under any circumstances, you miss the divine order of the Spirit. You have not to go back to law. You are in a new order. Law can only deal out one thing, and I will read what it deals in Hebrews 7:16: "Who is made, not after the law of a carnal commandment, but after the power of an endless life."

You never deal with law but you find it is a carnal commandment, always dealing with carnal things. It is always, "Thou shalt not."

There is no law to the Spirit. There never has been. You cannot find a law to Truth. The law has never had a place in a human body that has been filled with the power and the unction of the Holy Ghost. Law is done away, law is past. Life is begun, the new creation is formed, living after the new order. Christ being become the very principle of your human life and you no more touch law. You are above the law.

How many people are missing the greatest plan of the earth because they are continually trying to do something? My wife and I many years ago were strongly convinced on Sabbath Day holiness lines. We got so far that we thought it was wrong to have the milk man call, and it was a very fearful thing to ride in anything on a Sunday. We were so tightened up by the law that we were bound hand and foot.

There are thousands of people like that today. There are people that take up the new order of what they call the Seventh Day Adventists. But I want to tell you, you are touching miry clay when you touch anything on eating, drinking, or anything pertaining to the law. God would have you in a new order.

It is the law of the Spirit. It is a law of life. It is not a law of death and bondage.

As sure as you are in law you are in judgment and you judge everybody. Law is always judgment, and no one is right but those people who are keeping the law. They are full of judgment.

We have passed from death, from judgment, from criticism, from harshness, from hardness of heart.

> *Ye are our epistle,... known and read of all men..., And such trust have we through Christ to God-ward: not that we are sufficient of our selves to think anything as of ourselves; but our sufficiency is of God* —2 *Corinthians 3:2,4- 5*

Every person that begins thinking anything about himself

is touching human weakness. Just as you in any way try to please anybody, you are down. And you are very low down if you begin to worship anybody. No one must be worshipped.

When the glory appeared on the mount, as soon as it appeared and the disciples saw the whiteness, the brilliancy, the glory, the expression of the Master, and the very robes He wore becoming white and glistening, they began at once to think what they could do. Law will do it. What can we *do?* And they began doing, and they wanted to make three tabernacles, one for Moses, one for Elias, and one for Jesus. And then the cloud came. No person in the world has to be worshipped but the Lord. When the cloud lifted, there was no one seen but Jesus.

If you turn to anybody but Jesus, you will be law, you will be nature, you will be human.

It has always been so, people are always forming out things to do. What can I do? That is the reason why in the fourth chapter of Hebrews we read that the man that begins to do is a debtor to what he does. But the man that believes God, it is counted to him for righteousness — not doing but believing.

So God wants you to see that you have to cease from your doing, get away from it. Believe there is a spiritual vitality which shall bring into your very nature a new creation, which must be in the sons of God with power.

Interpretation of Tongues:

It is the Light that lighteth everyone that cometh into the world. It is the purity of the Son of God which is to bring us into a place where we will behold light in His light. It is the revelation from the Most High God. For in the old days men spoke as the prophets, but now in the last days God speaks to us by His Son.

His Son is in evidence, not the prophets but the Son. But if the prophets speak, as it will be, concerning the Son, then you will find the prophet position will be Amen to the Word of God.

> *Who also hath made us able ministers of the new testament; not of the letter, but of the spirit: for the letter killeth, but the spirit giveth life —2 Corinthians 3:6.*

In this new order, Jesus has one great plan for us, to fill us with the Holy Ghost that He should have a perfect focus in our human life, making all the displays of the brilliancy centered around the Son. And as we come into the light of this revelation by the Son, by the quickening of the Spirit, we will find our whole body regenerated with a new touch of divine favor, and we will think about spiritual things, and we will talk about spiritual things, and we will not touch anything that pertaineth to the flesh.

Interpretation of Tongues:

It is the light that dawneth just in the early morning and sets thy soul aglow with fervent heat of the light of the revelation of the Son, for whom He loveth He correcteth and changeth, and bringeth him to a desired heaven.

I love the dawning of the morning, breaking upon your soul with refreshing and keeping you in perfect order!

The Spirit or the Letter?

"The letter killeth, the spirit giveth life." Think about this very sincerely. Many people go very well for a time.

We have no trouble with the people that are getting baptized or seeking for the baptism or just when the Holy Ghost has touched them. All those three positions are lovely.

When are we troubled?

When the people cease to pursue and they turn aside and

spoil all that has been before, what's up? They were all right in the pursuit. They would have been all right continuing in the pursuit. There is not a place in the Scripture that you are ever allowed to drop the weapons which are spiritual attainment. You must see that you must denounce the powers of evil, the powers of darkness, the powers that would bring you into bondage. Denounce them all. You have been created now, filled now sustained in power. You go right on with God. Never turn again to the things 'round about you, setting your heart just upon Him as Jesus set His heart upon the cross.

There are three things which are wonderful: There is a good, there is a better, and there is a best.

After you have come into the fullness of the refreshing of God, you can get the letter instead of the life of the Word, and the letter will turn you to yourself, but the Spirit will turn you to Christ.

I say it without flinching, the people that have turned to water baptism in Jesus' name have turned away from a higher order of God. The people who have made Trinity Jesus have turned away from the "best" and they have "good." That's all they have got.

But there is a best. What is it? Not Spirit but the letter killeth. If they had gone on with God, the Spirit would have kept them in life. People turn away from the Spirit and take the letter, and when they get in the letter they are full of condemnation. Just as you live in the Spirit, there will be no condemnation in you. There is something wrong when you are the only one that is right. Just as the Church rises into the glory of the Lord and the vision of the Lord, will she be full of the love of the Lord?

The Holy Ghost wants you to sweep through darkness. The Holy Ghost wants to fill you with truth. The Holy Ghost wants to stimulate you in liberty. The Holy Ghost wants you to rise higher and higher.

What does the devil do? Try to get you to believe that you have some special revelation — some special revelation that is part truth. The devil never gives whole truth; he always gives part truth. What did the devil say? "If thou be the Son of God..." The devil knew that He was the Son of God.

I hear there is a place even in Los Angeles where they spend all their time in tongues. How ridiculous! How foolish! What's up? Letter. Turning away from the real truth of the Word of God.

God will shake this thing through you. If you turn away from the Word of God and won't have the Word, you will be judged by the Word of God and you will be brought into leanness.

Spiritual power will not have human attainment. The man that is living in the Spirit will not turn aside to please anybody. The man that is filled with the Spirit is going on with God all the time, and he will cease from his own works.

I am here to save you from ruts. I am here to stir your holy fidelity to know there is a place in the Holy Ghost that can keep you so that you do not get hard in the law, in judgment, in criticism, in hardness of heart. Get to a place where the Spirit has such a place with you that you will love to go God's way.

The judgment of God will begin at the house of God.

You have the best when you have the Spirit, and the Spirit brings life and revelation. Don't you turn to the law. Don't you turn to the natural. See to it that in the spiritual you are free from the law. The law of the Spirit is life to keep you out of death, to keep you out of judgment, to keep you out of bondage.

When Moses knew that he was bringing the tables of stone with the commandments down to the Israelite people, his heart was so full of joy. His whole body was so full, his whole countenance was so full that the people could not look upon him because of the glory that was expressed in his face. What was it? He was bringing liberty to the people, and it was law.

> But if the ministration of death, written and engraven in stones, was glorious, so that the children of Israel could not stedfastly behold the face of Moses for the glory of his countenance; which glory was to be done away: how shall not the ministration of the spirit be rather glorious? – 2 Corinthians 3:7-8.

If the law, which had with it life and revelation and blessing for Israel, could bring that wonderful exhibition of beauty and glory, what is it then if we are freed from the law and [have] the Spirit living, moving in us, without harshness, without "Thou shalt not," the Spirit of the Lord breathing through us and making us free from the law of sin and death?

Let us see to it that we get there.

For a moment I want to speak to you about the body. There are people in this place who want to be loosed in their minds, in their bodies, from their afflictions, loosed in every way.

You will never get loosed in the flesh. You will never get loosed in the letter. You will only get loosed as the Spirit of the Lord breathes upon the Word and you receive it as the life from the Lord, for the Word of the Lord is life. You receive the Word of the Lord just as it is and believe it, and you will find it quickens your whole body.

Any number of people are missing it because they are full of examination. You have to take the Word of God as the life of the Spirit, and you have to allow it to breathe through you, quickening your whole body for the Spirit quickeneth, but the flesh profiteth nothing.

The Word may be quick and powerful, or it may be deathlike. God wants us to be through with death. You are to be through with death and enter into death and keep in death till death is swallowed up with perfect victory of the perfect resurrection of the life of the Spirit that moves in you, quickening your mortal body.

The moment you turn from the spiritual health of this revelation of Christ, that moment you have ceased to go forward.

A man came to my meeting — he has been in these meetings. He was wonderfully blessed. He was a Wesleyan minister. He groaned, he travailed, he paid the price. Every time the Spirit came in, he went down and down and down into real death, and God quickened him by the Spirit.

So forcefully, so powerfully did the Spirit of the Lord breathe upon him, that he became like a flame of fire. He was in Vancouver. Every place became too small. Every place became enlarged. Money flowed in, thousands of dollars. Oh, the glory! Vancouver, looking at this young man, felt the glory, the expression of God flowing through his face, so beautiful.

But he was turning aside to baptizing in the name of Jesus. His glory departed. He lost everything he had, and then was shoved into a small theater. He lost everything.

What is it? Going back to letter, missing the summit, that glory that was upon him.

He wept and wept and wept, and said, "How can I get back?"

"Repent, Brother," I said, "Repent."

Some people are all the time covering the thing up when they know they are wrong. They won't repent. If you have gone off the line and gone the wrong way because people have said to go that way and left the first principles of the Christ of God, why not repent and get right. And I heard that he had repented...

(Interruption from the balcony): "Yes he has, Brother Wigglesworth, and he has gotten the victory too. Praise God!"

Oh, that is the man! God will restore you everything. When we repent, God restores.

Interpretation of Tongues:

It is of the depths, and where thou cannot trace and wonders come, and in the mystery of the wonderment, where two ways meet and thy heart cries and even thy nakedness appears in such a way that thou dost not know. Then in thy lowliness thou turneth again to the habitation of the Spirit and the Lord turns thy captivity and heals thy lands, and restores again to thee the vineyard and opens the heavens upon thee for blessing.

Oh! I see young men come into this work, I see people come into this work, and I know it is like opening the greatest door. Oh, what can happen! I see men passing through colleges. I see men clothed upon with abilities! Oh, how God can move them!

If I never went to school, if my mother and father never could read and write, and if I never went to school but my wife taught me to read, then I come to you just because the Holy Ghost has got my life. I come to you to help you. What can happen to a man that has been at the feet of Gamaliel and touched all the fullness of the fragrance of knowledge? What could God do if you let Him? Will you let Him?

Thou didst begin well. What hath hindered thee? Was it the Lord that came in the way? No, the Lord never stops your progress. It was some human thing. There was something that glittered, but it was not pure gold. There was something that shook thy confidence, but it was never God.

So I pray for you this morning, you mighty of the Lord,

you children of the Most High God, you people whom the Lord is looking upon with great favor. Believe that as the Holy Ghost moved upon Paul, moved upon the apostles, He can bring you forth as tried as gold and purified.

Will you believe? May the blessing of God, the Father, the Son, the Holy Ghost, fill you so that all the powers of hell shall not be able to prevail against you.

I had no thought of what has been going on this morning, but I do praise God. There has risen in my heart such love for this brother, and I have wept alone, very sorry, troubled, wondering what would be the outcome of it. I got three men to pray with me that we should bind the powers, that he should be loosed. He does not know anything about it. My daughter and I have gone before the Lord for him.

Oh, I do hope that the future shall be so mighty! Let us pray that God shall send him to Vancouver with this new thrill of holy life pressing through, till Vancouver will feel the warmth of heaven!

O God, we pray thee bless this dear soul. He has been heartbroken so long. He has been in great stress and trial for so long. O God, let the Holy Spirit rest upon him and move him for Vancouver, and let no power in the world interfere with his progress, in Jesus' name.

Now it is the glory side I am coming to. I want you to notice that there is an exceeding glory and it is only in the knowledge of the Lord Jesus.

> But if the ministration of death...was glorious...; which glory was to be done away

Was it ever thought possible that law could be done away? Yes, by something which is far more glorious.

There were three things in the old dispensation far different from three things in the new dispensation. Look at the old.

What is it the Lord thy God requireth of thee but thou shouldest do justly.

That is a thing that law was continually confronting them with. There was everybody out of order, and so the God of almightiness drew them to the place that the first thing necessary for them to know was how to do justly.

What doth the Lord thy God require of thee, but to love mercy...

In the law they had no mercy, and God brought this right into the midst of the law, a thing that they did not know how to do.

What doth the Lord thy God require of thee, but...to walk humbly with thy God.

The person that keeps the law never walks humbly, but is always filled with self-righteousness.

But now let the Spirit speak to us in the last days. What is it the Lord thy God desires of thee?

Thou shalt love the Lord with all thy heart.

Isn't that a new spiritual vision? That isn't the law; that is a boundless position. Law could never do it.

Thou shalt love the Lord thy God with all thy soul.

Thou shalt love the Lord thy God with all thy strength.

No reserve.

"Thou shalt love the Lord thy God with all thy mind" — with all of your pure mind serving the Lord.

The law had to be done away because, though it was glorious, it had to be exceeding in glory by a pure heart, by all strength for God.

Just fancy your knowing you are so created after the fashion of God that you want all the strength out of your food for God, all the strength. Just think of you people who have wonderful capabilities and wonderful minds, that your minds have to be all for God.

Glorious, more glorious! It is exceeding glory. Your own has to be done away. Nothing will put law away, only perfect love. There is no law to love. Love never had a law. It never had a sacrifice. If ever you talk about sacrifice, it means to say you do not know what it is to love.

For the joy that was set before Him, He endured the cross. "Cross is nothing to me. Death itself is nothing to me. All that they do is nothing. Oh, the joy I have of saving all the people of Los Angeles!"

Oh, this depth of the grace of the loftiness, of the holiness, of the sweetness!

Oh, this is like heaven to me,
This is like heaven to me;
I've crossed over Jordan
To Canaan's fair land,
And this is like heaven to me.

If you are in this love, you will be swallowed up with holy desire. You will have no desire, only the Lord. Your mind will be filled with divine reflection. Your whole heart will be taken up with the things that pertain to the kingdom of God, and you will live in the secret place of the Most High, and you will abide there.

Remember, it is abiding where He covers you with His feathers. It is a place of inner, inner, inner, inner, where you have moved outer and outer, altogether, and where the Lord now has the treasures.

There is an exceeding . There is a glory where you forget your poverties, where you forget your weaknesses, where you forget your human nature history and you go on to divine opportunity.

> *For if the ministration of condemnation be glory, much more doth the ministration of righteousness exceed in glory* —2 Corinthians 3:9

You see, it is a ministry of condemnation, is the law, and the Spirit is a ministry of righteousness. The difference is this: Instead of preaching to the people, "Thou shalt not" any more, you preach now that there is a superabundant position in the Holy One in the life of the Son, in the reflection by the Holy Ghost into the entirety of your whole heart, where He has come in and transformed the whole situation till every judged thing is past, life flows through, and you preach righteousness.

You will never get free by keeping the law, but if you believe in the blood, that will put you to death, you will have life divine, and you can sweep through the thing that binds you, because righteousness will abound where the law is of the Spirit.

The Jews will never have this light revealed to them until one thing happens. What is happening now? I have talked with rabbis. I have good times with them. I visit the synagogues and see good things there, and I have good times with these people.

When I was in Jerusalem on the platform with a number of Jewish rabbis, I had a chance. I had been preaching every place round about there. I had preached in the prison. I tell you, it was lovely to preach at the foot of Mount Carmel. It was very lovely for me to wake up and look across the Lake of Galilee and see that place where the demons came into the pigs and ran down the hill.

I had a good time there, but it was most glorious of all that last address for half an hour on a Jerusalem platform in front of all these judges, addressing these people from all over the country as the power of God fell upon me, with tears running down my face, telling about the Nazarene, the King of kings, the Lord of glory moving them to the Spirit instead of the law

It was glorious. They came around me afterward, and several of these Jews and one of the rabbis would ride with me in the train, and then when we got to Alexandra they would go with me to have some food.

"There is something about your preaching which is different from the rabbi," they said.

"Well, what is it?" I asked.

"Oh, you moved us! There was a warmth about it!"

"Yes, Brother. It wasn't law. The glory position is that it is warm. You feel it. It is regenerative. It is quickening. It moves your human nature. It makes you know that this is life divine.."

They listened round the table, and these Jews said, "Oh, but it is so different!"

"Yes," I said, "and the day is coming when your veil will be taken from your eyes and you will see this Messiah."

After dinner they said, "We have to leave. Oh, we do not feel we want to leave you!"

Ah, brethren, the Jews someday will be grafted in. The day of the Jews is coming. But oh, I don't want us Gentiles to miss the opportunity!

God wants us now so filled with the Spirit that we do not lose the glory by judging and harshness. We forget these things, and we press on to the prize of the mark of our high calling in Christ Jesus, and we see that we have received the life of the Spirit, which has quickened us, for "where the Spirit of the Lord is, there is liberty."

Liberty? What kind of liberty?

Liberty from glory to glory. Liberty of loosing you, till the very affection of the nature of the Son of God beings to be, till you are absorbed in this glory.

> *What is man, that thou art mindful of him, or the son of man that thou visitest him? Yet thou hast made him but a little lower than the angels, and hast clothed him with honor and glory.*

It is the Spirit that quickens; it is the Word that brings life. We want *you* to eat of the hidden manna. We do not want you to eat the sour grapes that turn the edge of your teeth. We want you to eat and be satisfied. Eat of that which is spiritual, quickening, and divine.

Gifts of Healing

The Holy Ghost people have a ministry. All the people which have received the Holy Ghost might be so filled with the Holy Ghost that without having the gift, the Holy Ghost within them brings forth healing power.

That is the reason why we say to you people, "Never be afraid of coming near me when I am praying for the sick." I love to have people help me. Why? Because I know there are people in this place who have a very dim conception of what they have got. I believe the power of the Holy Ghost which you have received has power so to bring you into concentration that you dare believe for God to heal apart from knowing you have a gift.

Now I deal with the gift. Gifts of healing, not gift of healing. There is a difference and we must give it the proper name.

Gifts of healing can deal with every case of sickness, every disease that there is. It is so full, beyond human expression, but you come into the fullness of it as the light reveals to you.

There is something about a divine healing meeting which may be different in some respects to others. I have people continually coming to me and saying, "When you are preaching, I see a halo about you. When you are preaching, I have seen angels standing 'round about you."

I am confronted from time to time about these things, and I am thankful for people to have vision. I do not have that kind of vision, but I have the express glory the glory of the Lord covering me, the intense inner working of His power, till every time I have stood before you I have known I have not had to choose language. The language has been chosen, the thoughts have been chosen, and I have been speaking in prophecy more than in any other way. So I know we have been in these days in the School of the Holy Ghost in a great way.

The only vision I have had in a divine healing meeting is this: So often I have put hands upon the people and I have seen two hands go before my hands many, many times.

The person that has the gifts of healing does not look. You will notice on the platform after I have got through, many things are manifested, but it doesn't move me. I am not moved by anything I see. I have never seen anything yet that is like what I have to see.

The divine gift of healing is so profound in the person that has it that there is no such thing as doubt and could not be, and whatever happens would not change the man's opinion or thought or act. He expects the very thing that God intends him to have as he lays hands upon the seeker.

Wherever I go the manifestation of divine healing is greater by ever so much in every way after I get away than when I am there. Why? God's plan for me. God has great grace over me. Wonderful things have been established and told as they happened when I was there, but were hid from me. God has a reason why He hides things from me.

When I lay hands upon people, I tell you that thing will take place. I believe it to be so, and I never turn my ear or my eyes from the fact. It has to be.

Divine healing — the gift of it — is more than audacity. It is more than an unction. Those are two big things. It is a rigid fact of a divine nature within the human man, pressing forward the very nature and act of the Lord if He were there. We are in this place for the glorifying of the Father, and the Father will be glorified in the Son as we are not afraid of acting in this day.

People sometimes come to me very troubled. They will say, "I had the gift of healing once, but something has happened and I do not have it now." You never had it. "Gifts and callings are without repentance" and they remain under every circumstance, only this: you fall from grace and use a gift wrongly, it will work against you. If you use tongues out of the will of God, interpretation will condemn you. If you have been used and the gift has been exercised and you have fallen from your high place, it will work against you.

The gift of the Holy Ghost, when He has breathed in you, will make you alive so that it is wonderful. It seems almost then as though you have never been born. The jealousy God has over us, the interest He has in us, the purpose He has for us, the grandeur of His glory are so marvelous – God has called us into this place to receive gifts.

Now I want to tell you how to receive a gift. The difference between the speaking in tongues by the gift and speaking in tongues by the Spirit is this: Everybody that is baptized speaks as the Spirit gives utterance, but this is not the gift. The gift is a special manifestation in the life that they know, and they could talk in tongues as long as they would. But the man or woman should never speak longer than the Spirit gives unction, should never go beyond, like the person giving prophecy he will never go beyond the spiritual unction.

The trouble is this: After we have been blessed with tongues, there is the natural thing. Everything that is not the rising tide of the Spirit is law or letter. What is law or letter? Law is that you have dropped into human order. Letter is that you are depending upon the Word without the power. These two things will work against you instead of working for you. The letter and the law bring harshness; the Spirit brings joy and felicity. One is perfect harmony; the other genders strife. One is higher tide; the other is earthly. The one gets into the bliss of the presence of heaven; the other never rises from earthly associations.

Claim your right. Claim your position. The man will never get a gift under any circumstances who asks for it twice. I am not moved by what you think about it. I believe this is sovereignty from God's altar. You never get a gift if you ask for it twice. But God will have mercy upon you if you stop asking and believe.

There is not a higher order that God has set on foot today over the person that believes than, "Ask and you shall receive." If you dare ask for any gift, if you really believe that it is a necessity gift, if you dare ask and will not move from it but begin to act in it, you will find the gift is there.

If you want to be in the will of God, you will have to be stubborn. What do you mean? Unchangeable. Do you believe if you got a gift you will feel it? Nothing like it. If you ask for a gift do not expect to have a feeling with it. There is something better. There is a fact with it, and the fact will bring the feeling, after the manifestation. People want feeling for gifts. There is no such thing. You will make the biggest mistake if you dare to pray on any line till you feel like doing anything. As sure as can be, you have lost your faith. You have to believe that after you receive you have the power and you begin to act in the power.

The next morning after I received the gift of tongues, I went out of the house with a box of tools on my back, going down the street to do some work. The power of God lit me up, and I broke out in tongues, loud, my they were loud. The street was filled with people and there were some gardeners trimming some hedges and cutting the grass. They stuck their heads over like swan necks.

"Whatever is up? Why, it is the plumber."

I said, "Lord, I am not responsible for this, and I won't go from this place till I have interpretation."

God knows I wouldn't move from that place. And out came interpretation. This was the interpretation: "Over the hills and far away before the brink of day the Lord thy God will send 'thee forth and prosper all thy way."

This is the point: The gift was there. I did not pray for it. I did not say, "Lord, give me the interpretation." I said, "If you don't give it to me, I won't move." And that meant to say that I was determined to have the gift.

It has been surprising, but at everyplace where I am, the Spirit of the Lord moves upon me.

I want to say something about the gift of interpretation, because it is so sublime, it is so divine, it is such a union with the Christ. It is a pleasing place with the Christ. It is not the Holy Ghost that is using it so much, but it is the Christ who is to be glorified in that act, for the Trinity moves absolutely collectively in the body.

As soon as that had taken place, wherever I went when anybody spoke in tongues I did not say, "Lord, give me the interpretation." That would have been wrong. I lived in a fact. Now, what is a fact? A fact is that which produces. Fact produces. Fact has it. Faith is a fact. Faith moves fear and faction. Faith is audacity. Faith is a personality. Faith is the living Christ manifested in the believer.

Now, what is interpretation? Interpretation is that which moves and brings forth without thought. If you are on the line of interpretation and if you get words before you are to them, that is not interpretation. The person who interprets does not have the words. The gift breathes forth, the person speaks on, never stops till he is through, and he says things that he does not know what he is saying till the words are out. He does not form them, he does not arrange for them. Interpretation is a divine flood, just as tongues is a flood. So it requires faith continually to produce this thing.

Now, I come back to the gift of healing. Gift of healing is a fact. It is a production. It is a faith. It is an unwavering trust. It is a confidence. It is a reliability. It knows it will be.

A divine gift has apprehension. It is also full of prophetic utterances There is no such thing as an end to the divine vocabulary.

What is faith? Is it an earnest? More. Is it a present? More. It is relationship. Are there better things than relationship? Yes. What is it? Sonship is relationship. But heirship is closer still, and faith is "God manifested in flesh."

"What was Jesus?" you ask. Jesus was the manifested glory in human incarnation.

Anything else? Yes. Jesus was the fullness of the express image of the Father.

Is that ours? Yes. Who are the chosen ones? They that ask and believe and see it done. God will make you chosen if you believe it.

Let us repent of everything that is hindering us. Let us give place to God. Let us lose ourselves in Him. Let us have no self-righteousness, but let us have brokenness, humbleness, submittedness. Oh, may there be today such brokenheartedness in us today. May we be dead indeed and alive indeed with refreshings of the presence of the Most High God!

Some of you have been saying, "Oh, I wish I could know how to get a gift." Some of you have felt the striving of the Holy Ghost pressing you through. Oh beloved, rise to the occasion this day. Believe God. Ask God for gifts, and it may come to pass in your life. But do not ask without you know it is the desire of your heart. God grant to us gifts and graces!

CHAPTER 6

Lake's Reply to Four Questions Concerning Healing
By John G Lake

THE SOUTHERN ASSOCIATION OF EVANGELISTS, who recently met at Hot Springs, Arkansas, in a convention, wrote as follows:

Rev. John G. Lake Spokane, Wash.

Dear Sir:

We are submitting the following questions to about twenty-five leading professors, preachers, and evangelists, for reply, and recognizing your extensive experience in the ministry of healing, trust that you will favor us with an early reply. The questions are as follows:

FIRST: Is God able to heal?
SECOND: Does God ever heal?

THIRD: Does God always heal?

FOURTH: Does God use means in healing?

MY REPLY

Question 1. Is God Able to Heal?

Coming as an inquiry from the Church of Christ in her varied branches, as represented by your association, which includes ministers and evangelists of almost every know sect, is a confession of how far the Modern Church has drifted in her faith from that of the Primitive Church of the first four centuries.

That this apostasy is true, may readily be seen by a study of the New Testament, together with the writings of the Christian fathers of the first centuries. That Jesus Himself healed All who came to Him; that the apostles after His resurrection and after the outpouring of the Spirit upon the Church on the day of Pentecost, continued to do the same, is a New Testament fact. It is well known that the Church fathers testified to the vast extent of the miracle-working power of Christ through His followers, until the day of Constantine.

With the establishment of Christianity as the state religion under Constantine, a flood of heathenism poured into the Church, and the vitality of the faith in Christ as Saviour and Healer disappeared. Hordes of unbelievers came into the Church with very slight knowledge of Christ, bringing with them many heathen customs and practices, some of which quickly predominated in the Church.

Among these was trust in MAN rather than Christ, as healer of the body.

That isolated saints of God and groups of Christians have trusted God exclusively, and proved Him the healer, is found in the experience of the Church in every century. Among those in modern times were the Hugenots of France, who excelled in their faith in God. Many of them were consciously baptized in the Holy Ghost, and history records that many of them spoke in tongues by the power of the Holy Spirit. The sick were healed through faith in Jesus Christ and the laying on of hands. Many prophesied in the Spirit.

The Coming of the Reformation

With the coming of Protestantism, and the establishment of the great churches of the present day, little knowledge of Christ as the Healer existed. Protestantism was established on one great principle, the revelation of Martin Luther, his watchword and slogan "The just shall live by faith." Not by works of penance, but through faith in the living, risen, glorified Son of God.

Isolated cases of healing are recorded by Luther, John Knox, Calvin, and Zewengle, and others of the reformers. With the birth of Methodism, under John Wesley, a fresh impetus was given to the teaching of healing through faith in Jesus. Wesley recorded in his journal, many instances of wonderful healings of the sick, of casting out of demons, and remarkable answers to prayer.

Healing In Modern Times

The modern teaching of healing received a new impetus through Doroth Trudell, a factory worker in one of the German provinces. Under her ministry many were healed, so that eventually the German Government was compelled to recognize her healing institution at Mennendorf and license it. During the present century a great number of men definitely taught and practiced the ministry of Divine Healing.

Among the writer on the subject of healing who are well

known to the Christian Church, are A. J. Gordon. Dr. A. B. Simpson, and Rev. Andrew Murray of South Africa.

Andrew Murrays Experience

The Rev. Andrew Murray's Experience in healing was as follows: He was pronounced incurable of a throat disease, known as "Preacher's Throat," by many London specialists. In despair he visited the Bethsan Divine Healing Mission in London, conducted by Dr. Bagster. He knelt at the altar, was prayed for by the elders, and was healed. He returned to South Africa, wrote and published a book on Divine Healing, which was extensively circulated in the Dutch Reform Church of South Africa, of which he was the recognized leading pastor. The effect of the book was to call the people's attention to the fact that Jesus is the Healer still. Great celebrations took place in the various churches of South Africa when Andrew Murray returned a living example of Christ's power and willingness to heal.

In a short time persons who read of his ministry of healing made request of their pastors to be prayed for, that they might be healed. In some instances the pastors confessed that they had no faith, and could not honestly pray with them for healing. Others made one excuse after another. Eventually the people began to inquire what was the trouble with their pastors. Andrew Murray, the chief pastor had been healed. He had written a book on healing. Members of the Church throughout the land were praying through to God, and finding Him their Healer still. But the preachers in general were confessing lack of faith. So the circulation of the book became an embarrassment to them. Instead of humbly confessing their need to God, and calling upon Him for that measure of the Spirit's presence and power that would make prayer for the sick answerable, they decided to demand the withdrawal of Andrew Murray's book from circulation in the Church, and this was done. Although the truth of the teaching of Divine Healing, and the personal experience in the healing of Andrew Murray, and hundreds of others through his ministry and the ministry of believers in the Church remained unchallenged, Rev. Andrew Murray was requested not to practice the teaching of Divine Healing in the Dutch Reform Church of South Africa.

This experience illustrates with clearness, the difficulties surrounding the introduction of a more vital faith in the living God in the Modern Church. Every Church has had, in a greater or lesser degree, a somewhat similar experience. The usual custom in the Modern Church is that when a preacher breaks out in a living faith and begins to get extraordinary answers to prayer, he is cautioned by the worldly wise, and if persistent, is eventually made to feel that he is regarded as strange. If he still persists, he is ostracized and actually dismissed by some churches and conferences.

Experiences like the above are entirely due to the failure of the Modern Church to recognize the varied ministries of the Spirit set forth in the New Testament. The Word in the 12th of Corinthians says concerning the order of ministers in the Church that: "God hath set some in the church, first apostles, secondarily prophets, thirdly teachers, and after that miracles, then gifts of healing, helps, government, diversities of tongues." Thus a ministry for every man called of God is provided. No one conflicting with the other. All recognized as equally necessary to the well-rounded body of Christ.

The Modern Church must come to a realization of other ministries in the Church besides preaching. In the Modern Church the preacher is the soul and center and circumference of his church. The Primitive Church was a structure of faith composed of men and women, each qualifying in his or her particular ministry. One ministered in the healing of the sick, another a worker of miracles, another a teacher of the ways and the will of God, another an evangelist, another a pastor, another an overseer.

It should be an easy matter for any modern Church to adopt itself to adapt itself to the gifts of the Spirit and so remove forever the difficulty that befell the Dutch Reform Church in South Africa, and has befallen our own churches. Instead of discouraging a ministry of the Spirit through the practice of varied gifts in the Church, these ministries and powers may be conserved and utilized for the building of the kingdom.

The Church at Spokane

A little over five years ago, we established in Spokane, Divine Healing Rooms with a competent staff of ministers. They believed in the Lord as the present, perfect Healer, and ministered the Spirit of God to the sick through prayer and the laying on of hands. The records show that we ministered up to 200 persons a day: that of these, 176 were non-church members. The knowledge of and faith in Jesus Christ as the Healer, has griped the world outside of the present Church society, and the numbers of those who believe are increasing with such rapidity that in a short time they may become a majority in many communities.

Question II. Does God Ever Heal?

The New Testament records forty-one cases of healing by Jesus, Himself. In nine of these instances not only were the individuals healed, but multitudes, and in three instances it especially say "great multitudes."

With the growth of His life's work, the demand for extension was imperative, and in Luke 9, we read: "Jesus called his twelve disciples together, and gave them power and authority over all devils, and to cure diseases, and he sent them to preach the kingdom of God and to heal the sick."

When they in turn were overwhelmed with work we read in Luke 10, that Jesus appointed Seventy others also, and sent them into the cities round about, saying, "Heal the sick that are therein, and say unto them, The Kingdom of God is come nigh unto you."

If there were any foundation whatever for the foolish belief that only Jesus and the apostles healed, the appointment of these Seventy should settle it. When the Seventy returned from their evangelistic tour, they rejoiced saying, "Master, even the demons were subject to thy name."

In addition to the Seventy we read that the disciples complained to Jesus, saying: "We saw one casting out devils in thy name; and we forbad him, because he followeth not with us." And Jesus replied, "Forbid him not: for no man shall do a miracle in my name that can lightly speak evil of me. He that is not against us is for us."

This then makes a New Testament record of eighty-four persons who healed during the life-time of Jesus. Jesus, the twelve apostles, seventy others, and the man who "followeth not with us."

Paul and Barnabas were not apostles during the lifetime of Jesus, but we read in the Acts, of their healing many. Paul himself was healed through the ministry of Ananias, an aged disciple, who was sent to him through a vision from the Lord.

Philip was one of the evangelists who preached at Samaria, and under his ministry there were remarkable signs and wonders.

Under the ministry of the Apostle Paul, the sick were not only healed, and the dead raised, but handkerchiefs were brought to the apostle, that they might contact his person. When laid upon the sick, the disease disappeared and the "demon departed from them."

The Book of James gives final and positive instructions of what to do in case of sickness.

Commanding that if sick, one shall send for the elders of the Church. Concerning their prayer of faith the Word says: "The prayer of faith shall save the sick, and the Lord shall raise him up; and if he have committed sins they shall be forgiven him."

The great number of medieval miracles, deserve respectful treatment and the cumulative evidence of so much concurrent testimony by distinguished and upright men makes it impossible to think that they were all deluded and mistaken.

Ministry of Dr. John Alexander Dowie

During the life of John Alexander Dowie, and before his mentality was affected through overwork, he established a city in the state of Illinois, forty miles north of Chicago, on the lake shore, known as Zion City. The city was established in 1901. In twelve months it had a population of 4000. In three years the population was estimated at ten thousand. The city Council passed by-laws banishing drugs, medicine, and the use of swine's flesh. None of these are used by his followers if they wish to remain in good standing. Their vital statistics reveal their death rate is lower than that of other cities of the same population. Insurance companies were afraid to insure the Zion people because of the well-known fact that they would not employ physicians or medicine. But at present, insurance companies are seeking their business. They are recognized to be among the healthiest people in the United States.

On an occasion at the Chicago Auditorium, persons from all parts of the world who had been healed through his ministry, were invited to send testimonies on a card 2&1/2 by 4&1/2 inches. It required five bushel baskets to hold these cards. They numbered sixty thousand. Ten thousand in the audience rose to their feet testifying to their own personal healing by the power of God, making grand total of Seventy thousand testimonies.

In South Africa, Divine Healing holds such sway among both black and white, that army officers estimated that in the recent war, twenty out of every hundred refused medical aid, and trusted God only. This necessitated in the army the establishment of a Diving Healing Corps, which ministered healing by the Spirit of God.

Among prominent physicians who have not only been healed of God, but have adopted the ministry of healing through faith in the Lord Jesus Christ are: Phneas D. Yoakum of Los Angeles, head of the Pisgah Institution, whose blessed ministry of healing is recognized by Christians everywhere. Dr. William To, Gentry of Chicago, who was not only prominent in his profession as physician, but as the author of Materia Medica in twenty volumes, to be found in every first-class medical library. His publisher sold over 100,000 copies of this work.

To this I add my personal testimony, after twenty-five years in the ministry of healing, that hundreds of thousands of sick have been healed of the Lord, during this period, through churches and missionary societies founded on the pattern of the Primitive Church, finding God's equipment of power from on high.

With this weight of testimony before us, it seems childish to continue debating the ability or willingness of God to heal the sick. Let us rather with open minds and heart receive the Lord Jesus Christ, as Saviour and Healer, and trust Him with our bodies as we trust Him with our souls.

Question III. Does God Always Heal?

In considering the subject of Divine Healing and its

applicability to present day needs, the question, "Does God Always Heal?" is uppermost. The Church at large has taught that healing is dependent on the exercise of the Will of God, and that the proper attitude of the Christian to assume is, "If it be thy will." Continuously we hear men say, "No doubt God can heal; He has the power, and He can heal if He will."

We believe that this attitude of mind and this character of reasoning is due to the ignorance of the plain Word and Will of God, as revealed through Jesus Christ. We contend that God is always the Healer. We contend further that it is not necessary for God to will the healing or non-healing of any individual. In His desire to bless mankind, He willed once and for all and forever that man should be blessed and healed. He gave Jesus Christ as a Gift to the world, that this blessing might be demonstrated and His willingness and desire to heal forever made clear.

Christians readily admit that Jesus is the entire expression of the Law and the Life and the Will of God. As such, He demonstrated forever by His words and acts, what the mind of God toward the world is. He healed all who came to Him, never refusing a single individual, but ever bestowed the desired blessing. In healing all and never refusing one, He demonstrated forever the willingness of God to heal all. He healed because it was the nature of God to heal, not because it was a caprice of the mind of God, or because the mind of God was changed toward the individual through some special supplication.

Whosoever was ready and willing to receive healing received it from the Lord. His grief in one instance is expressed in the Gospel narrative in that, "He could do there (in Nazareth) no mighty works because of their unbelief, save that he healed a few sick folk."

Men have assumed that it is necessary to persuade God to heal them. This we deny with all emphasis. God has manifested through Christ, His desire to bless mankind. His method of saving the world, and what constitutes His salvation, is shown in Matthew 4:23: "Jesus went about all Galilee, teaching in their synagogues, (revealing the Will of God) and preaching the gospel of the kingdom, and healing all manner of sickness and all manner of disease among the people."

The Parallel of the Dynamo

The method by which men receive the healing power is parallel to the method by which we light our homes through the use of electricity. A dynamo is set up. Through its motion, it attracts to itself the quality know as electricity. Having attracted electricity, it is then distributed through the wires wherever man will and our homes are lighted thereby. The dynamo did not make the electricity. It existed from time immemorial. It was the discovery of the ability to control electricity that made lighting of our homes a possibility. Without it, we would still be living by the light of a tallow candle or a kerosene lamp.

In the spiritual world, the spirit of man is the dynamo. It is set in motion by prayer, the desire of the heart. Prayer is a veritable Holy Spirit controlling dynamo, attracting to itself the Spirit of God. The spirit of God being received into the spirit of man through prayer, is distributed by the action of the will wherever desire. The Spirit of God flowed through the hands of Jesus to the ones who were sick, and healed them. It flowed from His soul, wirelessly, to the suffering ones and healed them also.

The Holy Spirit is this shown to be the universal presence of God, God omnipresent. The Spirit of God is given to man for his blessing, and is to be utilized by him to fulfill the Will of God.

The Will of God to save a man is undisputed by intelligent

Christians. The Will of God to heal every man is equally God's purpose. God has not only made provisions that through the Spirit of God received into our lives, our souls may be blessed and our bodies healed, but further, we in turn are expected and commanded by Jesus to distribute the Spirit's power to others, that they likewise may be healed and blessed.

The Spirit of God is ours to embrace. It is ours to apply to the need of either soul or body. Through Christ's crucifixion and through His victory over the grave, Jesus secured from the Father the privilege of shedding the Holy Spirit abroad over the world. This was the crowning climax of the redemptive power of God ministered through Jesus Christ to the world. And from this day to this, every soul is entitled to embrace to himself this blessed Spirit of God, which Jesus regarded so valuable to mankind, so necessary to their health and salvation, that He gave His life to obtain it.

Consequently it is not a question, "Does God always heal?" That is childish. It is rather a question, "Are we willing to embrace His healing?" If so, it is for us to receive. More than this it is for all the world to receive, for every man to receive, who will put his nature in contact with God through opening his heart to the Lord. Jesus knowing the world's need of healing, provided definitely for physicians (disciples, ministers, elders, those with the Gifts of Healing) who would minister, not pills and potions, but the power of God. The Gifts of Healing is one of the nine Gifts of the Spirit provided for and perpetuated forever in the Church (1 Corinthians 12:8-11). The Word says: "Jesus Christ the same yesterday, and today, and forever." Consequently there is healing from every disease, for every man who will in faith embrace the Spirit of God, promised by the Father, and ministered through Jesus Christ, to the souls and bodies of all who desire the blessing.

Peter in his exposition of this fact, says, "By whose stripes ye were healed." The use of "were" in this text indicates that the healing was accomplished in the mind of God when Jesus Christ gave Himself as the eternal Sacrifice, and has never had to be done over again for the healing of any individual. He willed it once; it is done forever. It is yours to have, yours to enjoy, and yours to impart to others.

Question IV. Does God Use Means in Healing?

By the term "means" is understood the varied remedies, medicines and potions commonly used by the world at large and prescribe for the sick—in short, Materia Medica. This should be an extremely easy question for anyone to decide. The world has always had her systems of healing. There were one thousand and one systems of healing evolved in all the centuries. They were mankind's endeavor to alleviate suffering. They existed in the days of Jesus, just as they exist today. The ancient Egyptians used them and were as proficient in the practice as our modern physicians. Indeed their knowledge of chemistry in some respects seem to have superseded ours, as they were able to produce an embalming substance that preserved the human body and kept it from dissolution.

The public commonly believes that medicine is a great science, and that its practice is entirely scientific. Whereas, so great a man as Professor Douglas McGlaggen, who occupied the chair of Medical Jurisprudence in the University of Edinborough, Scotland, declared: "There is no such thing as the science of medicine. From the days of Hippocrates and Galen until now we have been stumbling in the dark, from diagnosis to diagnosis, from treatment to treatment."

Dr. John B. Murphy, the greatest surgeon our country has

ever produced, has spoken his mind concerning surgery as follows: "Surgery is a confession of helplessness. Being unable to assist the diseased organ, we remove it. If I had my life to live over again, I would endeavor to discover preventative medicine, in hope of saving the organ instead of destroying it."

Just prior to his death he wrote an article entitled "The Slaughter of the Innocents," condemning cutting out of tonsils and adenoids, demonstrating that the presence of inflammation and pus and the consequent enlargement was due to a secretion in the system that found lodgment in the tonsils and that the removal of the tonsils in no way remedied the difficulty, the poison being generated in the system. He purposed to give his knowledge to the public for its protection from useless operations that he regarded criminal.

God's Contrast to Man's Way

What then, did Jesus have in mind as better than the world's system of healing, which He never used or countenanced? God's remedy is a Person and not a thing. The remedy that Jesus ministered to the sick was a spiritual one. It was the Holy Spirit of God. The tangible, living quality and nature of the living God, ministered through the Soul and Hands of Jesus Christ to the sick one.

So conscious was the woman who was healed of the issue of blood, that she had received the remedy, and of its effect and power in her, upon only touching the hem of His garment, that she "felt in her body that she was made whole of that plague." Jesus likewise was aware of the transmission of the healing power, for He said, "Someone hath touched me, for I perceive virtue has gone out of me."

That same virtue was ministered through the hands of the apostles and of the Seventy. It was also ministered by the early Christians, when they received from God, through the Holy Ghost, the ability to minister the Spirit of God to others. Of the twelve apostles it is said: "He gave them power and authority over all devils, and to cure diseases. And He sent them to preach the kingdom of God, and to heal the sick." Luke 9:1-2.

Of the Seventy it is written, "He sent them two and two, before his face into every city and place, whither he himself would come, and said unto them... 'Heal the sick that are therein, and say unto them, the kingdom of God is come nigh unto you.'"

So vital was this living Spirit of God and its healing virtue in the lives of the early Christians, that it is recorded of Paul that they brought handkerchiefs and aprons to him, that they might touch his body, and when these were laid upon the sick they were healed and the demons went out of them (Acts 19). In this instance even inanimate objects, handkerchiefs and aprons, were receptacles for the Spirit of God, imparted to them from the person of the Apostle Paul.

This was not an experience for the early Christian alone, but is the common experience of men and women everywhere who have dared to disbelieve the devil's lie, so carefully fostered and proclaimed by the church at large, that the days of miracles are past.

Every advanced Christian, who has gone out into God, who has felt the thrill of His Spirit, who has dared to believe that the Son of God lives by the Spirit in his life today, just as He lived in the lives of the early Christians, has found the same pregnant power of God in himself. Upon laying his hands in faith upon others who are sick, take place, and realized the transmission of Divine Virtue. Today millions of men and women trust God only, for the healing of their body from every character and forms of disease.

What, then, is this means of healing that Jesus gave as a

divine gift to Christianity, forever? It is the living Holy Spirit, ministered by Jesus Christ to the Christian soul, transmitted by the Christian because of this faith in the Word of Jesus, through his soul and his hands to the one who is sick. This reveals the law of contact in the mind of Jesus when He gave the commandment: "They shall lay hands on the sick, and they, shall recover." Mark 16:18.

With praise to God we record to His glory, that through twenty-five years in this ministry we have seen hundreds of thousands of persons in many parts of the world, healed by the power of God.

Throughout these twenty-five years, in different lands, we have established churches and societies composed of Christian men and women who know no remedy but the one Divine Remedy, the Lord Jesus Christ. They have faith in His redemption and in the presence and power of the Spirit of Christ to destroy sin and sickness in the lives of men forever.

In our own city, for five years, no day has passed in which we have not seen the healing of many.

For five years we have ministered, with our associate pastors, in The Church of Spokane alone, to an average of from one hundred and fifty to two hundred sick per day, who come from all quarters of the land, and even from foreign countries, to receive the healing power of God. These healings have included almost every known form of disease.

The majority of these healings have been of persons pronounced hopeless by their physicians.

Many of them had spent their all, some tens of thousands of dollars, for doctors, medicine, and operations. They found the Lord Jesus Christ, and the ministry of healing by the power of God, just as efficacious today as it ever was, thereby demonstrating the truth of the Word of God.

CHAPTER 7

Neglect Not the Gift that is in Thee
By Maria Woodworth-Etter

IN THE TENTH CHAPTER OF LUKE we read that the Lord appointed the seventy and sent them forth two and two before His face. He said, "Behold, I send you forth as lambs;" let us remain lambs and not become wolves to bite and snatch and tear and antagonise everybody. "Behold, I send you forth as lambs among wolves," but remember the wolves won't devour you. "Carry neither purse nor scrip." Don't be over-anxious about anything.

Verse 19: "Behold, I give you power to tread on serpents and scorpions, and over all the power of the enemy; and nothing shall by any means hurt you."

Then He tells them not to rejoice because they had power over the spirits, but rather rejoice that they are children of God. Don't be puffed up by the miracles, don't get your eyes on them, but keep your eyes on Jesus. You are not saved by miracles. You are saved and kept by the power of God. The miracles are the work of the Holy Ghost. You

89

will get a reward for the works of the Holy Ghost that are wrought through you, they are going to make your crown, but they will never save you.

If a hundred thousand were healed through my prayers a day, I could not pin my salvation to that. We are not saved by works, but through faith in Jesus, through living, constant faith and prayer. We are kept by the power of God. The works are thrown in and there will be a great reward for them; our crown will be the brighter.

Like Days of Old

Now in Moses' day the work was great as it is now, and the time came when the force of workers had to be enlarged. The Lord told Moses to select seventy men of good report, elders of the people, and bring them together to the tent of meeting that he might take of the Spirit that was upon Moses and put it upon them.

He said that they should be used in the same way as Moses; and so it was, the Spirit that rested on Moses came upon the seventy and they all began to prophesy. Then they were sent out to work. When the Spirit of God comes on you, you are not going to sit around idle and do nothing. And the Spirit fell upon two men who had stayed in the camp. They had not been brought into the tent by Moses, yet the Spirit fell upon them.

That made some feel jealous, and you will find the same spirit today, jealousy of those who are being blessed. Are you jealous for the cause or jealous for yourself? It wasn't for God's glory that Joshua asked Moses to forbid the prophesying of these men.

Thank God for Moses' answer, "Would that all the Lord's people were prophets." You must have the Spirit resting upon you if you are to do anything for God, either at home or abroad. You are not fit for work unless you have

Him, and those who serve at home must have Him the same as those who go to China or Africa.

God is not calling everyone to the foreign field, but God is calling everyone in some way. Many make the mistake of going out whom God has not called, and many spend all their time running around to camp meetings. Let us make every place a tent of meeting with the Lord and the Spirit may fall on us as on Eldad and Medad, who were not called to the tent of meeting.

And if you are not called to the foreign field, get to work in the place in which God does call you to labour. The hardest place God sends you to is just the place where He is going to give the greatest victory. But if you have not the Spirit and power of the Holy Ghost to energise you, you will be stranded.

God expects us to be qualified by the Spirit resting upon us even more in these last days than in the time of Moses. The seventy that Christ sent out had power, and how much more should we have power now that Christ is glorified? So we are expected to do all these great things set forth in the last chapter of Mark. Now in the 24th chapter of Matthew it says this Gospel of the kingdom shall be preached to all nations as a witness and then shall the end come. Friends, you and I cannot go out and preach as we used to do. Many sermons that God wonderfully blessed in the past I cannot preach now.

It is not so much in the might of preaching but in the demonstration of the Spirit. Sinners are more hard-hearted than they used to be. You can preach hell until they see the blaze, and yet they will stand and look you calmly in the face; but let them see the mighty power of God manifested and they are convicted. The disciples came to Jesus privately and asked Him what should be the sign of His coming and of the end of the world, and He answered these questions. The same questions are being asked today: "How will people know when He is coming back again? And then what will be the sign of the end when the tribulation is over?"

Now, we are given signs that we may know Jesus is coming soon. He goes on to tell many things that will happen by which we may know. He says this Gospel must be preached all over the world as a witness, and then shall the end come. This is our business, to sound the midnight cry, to herald the King. It is our mission to blow the trumpet in Zion among the saints, for the day of the Lord is at hand. It is near, even at the door, Jesus says in the same chapter, "Now from the fig tree learn her parable; when the branch putteth forth its leaves ye know that the summer is nigh; even so ye also, 'when ye see all these things know that He is nigh, even at the doors."

The Lord showed me last night, as I lay awake the most of the night, to gather together the ministers as far as I could, that we might see eye to eye, preach the same Gospel and have the same signs following. The word is going forth and the multitude is going to take it up and publish it everywhere, this Gospel of the kingdom, our last commission. So you see the saints going out to give this last message, telling the people that Jesus is coming soon.

Our Lord told us, as it was in the days of Noah so shall it be in our day. While the great mass of people are busy with the affairs of life a little band like Noah and his family are preparing to be hidden away in Christ from the disaster that will come upon the world. And we are told in the "time of the end" the book of Daniel will be read and understood. Daniel had called upon God to show him the future, and he was given a vision of great things taking place; but the Lord said, "It is not for this people, Daniel. It is for the people you ask about in the 'time of the end.' Seal up the book; they won't know anything about it now."

The book of Daniel is for our time and God is now opening His word. The light of heaven is shining upon us; God is unveiling it to us. He is giving us light on these things as never before. He says positively, " They that be wise shall understand." We are going to know before Jesus comes. Nearly everyone that is carried away in a vision gets the message, "Jesus is coming soon. Tell the people to be ready."

God expects us as ambassadors, as teachers, as messengers of His Kingdom to blow the trumpet that sounds the alarm to those who are not ready for His coming. He expects us to prove by His word, and by signs and wonders following our ministry, to make it plain that Jesus is coming soon.

We are going out to lift up Jesus. Paul says preaching has to be with demonstration of the Spirit and of power. The Holy Ghost bears witness with signs and miracles; unless these attend our ministry we cannot succeed.

There are scores and hundreds getting saved. They come from all parts of the country to get healed. The ministry of healing brings people more than anything else, and if you can lay hands on the sick and they recover, you will not have to preach to empty seats. You "produce the goods" of heaven, and people want the goods. Let the word go forth in demonstration and power so people can see what God has for them. There will be no failure in your ministry when they see the power of the Lord present to heal.

The main thing to keep before the people is the near coming of Jesus. We are not to set the day, God forbid; but the saints will know as the day draws nigh. We can tell by the signs that it is near. God expects you to preach as one having authority. This is a generation that will go up without dying. Christ looked down the age to our day and saw the whole world in unbelief, men fainting and their hearts failing them for fear of the things that were coming upon the earth, and

Daniel prophesied and said the wicked should grow worse and worse and none of the wicked should understand; but the wise shall understand.

We know the darkness of hell is spreading over this earth, and it will soon be a fearful scene, a regular deluge of blood. We have to sound the alarm and give the message that the King is coming. Some will be accounted worthy to escape all these things and stand before the Son of Man.

CHAPTER 8

The Hour is Come
By Smith Wigglesworth

YES, *I BELIEVE!* Oh, that our hearts and minds this day might come to that place of understanding, where we realize that it is possible, if we "only believe," for God to take all our human weaknesses and failures and transform us by His mighty power into a new creation. What an inspiration to give God the supreme place in our lives; when we do, He will so fill us with the Holy Spirit that the government will rest upon His shoulders. Oh, to believe, and come into the holy realm of the knowledge of what it means to yield our all to God. Just think of what would happen if we only *dared to believe God!* Oh, for a faith that *leaps* into the will of God and says, Amen!

COMMUNION PREPARATIONS

There is no service so wonderful to me as the service of partaking of the Lord's supper, the holy communion. The Scriptures say, *"As oft as ye do it, ye do it unto me"* - you do it in remembrance of Him. I am sure that every person in this place has a great desire to do something for Jesus; and that which He wants to do, is to keep in remembrance the cross, the grave, the resurrection, and the ascension, for the memory of these four events will always bring you into a place of great blessing. You do not need, however, to continually live on the cross, or even in remembrance of the cross, but what you need to remember about the cross is, *"It is finished."* You do not need to live in the grave, but only keep in remembrance that "He is risen" out of the grave, and that we are to be "seated with Him in glory."

> *Then came the day of unleavened bread, when the passover must be killed. And He sent Peter and John, saying, Go and prepare us the passover, that we may eat. —Luke 22:7-8*

The institution of the holy communion is one of those settings in Scripture, a time in the history of our Lord Jesus Christ, when the mystery of the glories of Christ was being unveiled. As the Master trod this earth, how the multitudes would gather with eagerness and longing in their hearts to hear the words that dropped from His gracious lips; but there were also those who had missed the vision. They saw the Christ, heard His words, but those wonderful words were to them like idle tales. When we *miss the vision* and do not come into the fulness of the ministry of the Spirit, there is a cause. Beloved, there is a *deadness* in us that must have the resurrection touch. Today we have the unveiled truth, for the dispensation of the Holy Ghost has come to unfold the fulness of redemption, that we might be clothed with power; and that which brings us into the state where God can pour upon us His blessing, is a *broken spirit and a contrite heart.* We need to examine ourselves this morning to see what state we are in, whether we are just "religious" or whether we be truly "in Christ."

The human spirit, when perfectly united with the Holy Spirit, has but one place, and that is death, death, and deeper death. The human spirit will then cease to desire to have its own way, and instead of "my" will, the cry of the heart will be, "Thy will, oh, Lord, be done in me."

> *And he sent Peter and John, saying, Go and prepare us the passover, that we may eat. And they said unto him, Where wilt thou that we prepare? And he said unto them, Behold, when ye are entered into the city, there shall a man meet you, bearing a pitcher of water; follow him into the house where he entereth in. And ye shall say unto the goodman of the house, The Master saith unto thee, Where is the guestchamber, where I shall eat the passover with my disciples? And he shall shew you a large upper room furnished: there make ready. —Luke 22:8-12*

It is one thing to handle the Word of God, but it is another thing to "believe" what God says. The great aim of the Spirit's power within us is to so bring us in line with His perfect will that we will unhesitatingly believe the Scriptures, daring to accept them as the authentic divine principle of God. When we do, we will find our feet so firmly fixed upon the plan of redemption that it will not matter from whence come trials or other things, for our whole nature will be so enlarged, that it will be no more I, but, "Lord, what wilt thou have me to do?"

Every believer should be a living epistle of the Word, one who is "read and known of all men." Your very presence should bring such a witness of the Spirit that everyone with whom you come in contact would know that you are a "sent" one, a light in the world, a manifestation of the Christ; and last of all, that you are a "biblical" Christian.

Those disciples had to learn that whatever Jesus said must come to pass. Jesus said, very slowly, I believe, and thoughtfully, "When you go into the city, there shall a man meet you bearing a pitcher of water. Follow him into the house, and just when he has entered in, say, the Master hath need of a room where he may eat the passover with his disciples." That is the way that Jesus taught them. Beloved, let me say this: *There is no person in Palestine who has ever seen a "man" bearing a pitcher of water.* It is a thing unknown. Therefore, we find Jesus beginning with a prophecy which brought that inward knowledge to them that what He said must come to pass. This is the secret of the Master's life — *prophecy which never failed.* There is no power that can change the Word of God. Jesus was working out this great thought in the hearts of His disciples, that they might *know* that *"it shall come to pass."*

After Jesus had given that wonderful command to Peter and John, those disciples were walking into the city, no doubt in deep meditation, when suddenly they cried out in amazement, "Look! There He is! Just as the Master hath said."

When in Jerusalem I was preaching on Mount Olivet, and as I looked down, at my right hand I saw where the two ways met, where the ass was tied. I could see the Dead Sea, and all the time I was preaching I saw at least 150 women going down with vessels and then carrying them back on their heads full of water; but, *not one man.* However, Jesus said that it had to be a "man," and so it was, for no one could change His word. Some have said to me that He had it all arranged for a man to carry a pitcher of water. I want to tell you that God does not have to arrange with mortals to carry out His plans. If He has the power to hear the cry of some poor needy child of His who may be suffering, and that one may be in England, Africa, China, or anywhere else, saying, "Oh, God, Thou knowest my need," and here in New York, Germany, California, or some other place, there is a disciple of His on his knees, and the Lord will say unto that one, "Send help to that brother or sister, and do not delay it," - and the help comes. He did not need to get a man to help Him out by carrying a pitcher of water. *According to His Word He worketh,* and Jesus said a "man" should carry water.

What did those disciples do as they saw the man - go forward to meet him? No, they waited for the man, and when he came up they probably walked alongside of him, without a word, until he was about to enter the house; and then I can hear one saying to him, "Please, Sir! The Master wants the guestchamber!"

"The guestchamber? Why, I was preparing it all day yesterday but did not know whom it was for."

With man things are impossible, but God is the unfolder of the mysteries of life, and He holds the universe in the hollow of His hand. What we need to know this morning is that ,"The Lord in the midst of thee is mighty," and He works according to His Word.

> *And when the hour was come, he sat down, and the twelve apostles with him. And he said unto them, "With desire I have desired to eat this passover with you before I suffer: For I say unto you, I will not any more eat thereof, until it be fulfilled in the kingdom of God." And he took the cup, and gave thanks, and said, Take this, and divide it among yourselves: For I say unto you, "I will not drink of the fruit of the vine, until the kingdom of God shall come." And he took bread, and gave thanks, and brake it, and gave unto them, saying, "This is my body which is given for you: this do in remembrance of me." —Luke 22:14-19*

It takes the Master to bring the Word home to our hearts. His was a ministry that brought a new vision to mankind, for "never man spake as He spake." How I love to hear Him preach. How He says things. I have watched Him as He trod this earth. Enter into the Scriptures and watch the Lord, follow Him, take notice of His counsel, and you will have a story of wonders. The Book speaks today! It is life, and looms up full of glory. It reflects and unfolds with a new creative power. The words of Jesus are life - never think they are less. If you believe it you will feel quickened. The Word is powerful; it is full of faith. *The Word of God is vital!* Listen! "The word profited them nothing because it was not mixed with faith in them that heard it" (Hebrews 4:2). There has to be a "hearing" in order to have faith. Faith is established and made manifest as we "hear" the Word. Beloved, read the Word of God in quietude, and read it "loud," so that you can "hear" it - for "He that *heareth* my word," to them it giveth life.

Beloved, listen! "With desire" - the "hour is come!" He speaketh! From the beginning of time there has never been an hour like this. These words were among the greatest that He ever spoke: *"The hour is come!" What* an hour, for, the *end of time had come.* "What?" you ask. Yes, I repeat it, for the redemption of the cross, the shedding of the blood, brought in a "new" hour. Time was finished and eternity had begun for a soul that was covered with the blood. All people lived but to die until "that" hour, but the moment the sacrifice was made, it was not the end, but only the beginning. Time was finished and eternity had begun. The soul that is covered with the blood has moved from a natural to an eternal union with the Lord, and then the commandment, *"Thou shalt not,"* which had so worried the people and brought them into such dissatisfaction because they could not keep the Law, was changed into a new commandment; and it was no more, "Thou shalt not," but, " I *delight to do thy will, oh, God."*

"All in Adam died," but now the "hour is come" and "all in Christ shall be made alive." Not death, but the fulness of life divine.

"I have a desire to eat this passover with you before I suffer. I know that within a few moments the judgment hall awaits me." Beloved, do you think that I could be in Jerusalem and not want to pass through the gate that He went through? Do you think that I could be in Jerusalem and not want to pass over the Brook Kedron? Could you imagine me being in Jerusalem and not want to go into the Garden, or view the tomb where His body was laid? I knelt down at that holy place, for I felt that I must commune with my Lord there.

While in Jerusalem, I preached many weeks outside the Damascus Gate, and God mightily blessed my ministry. It is wonderful to be in the place where God can use you. As I was leaving Jerusalem, some Jews who had heard me preach wanted to travel in the same compartment with me, and they wanted to stay at the same hotel where I was staying. Sitting around the table having food, they said, "What we cannot understand is, when you preach we feel such power; you 'move' us. There is something about it that we cannot help but feel that you have something different from what we have been used to hearing. Why is it?" I replied that it was because I *preached Jesus* in the power of the Holy Spirit, for He was the Messiah, and He causes a child of His to so live in the reality of a clear knowledge of Himself that others know and feel His power. It is this knowledge that the Church today is very much in need of.

Beloved, do not be satisfied with anything less than the knowledge of a real change in your nature, a knowledge of the indwelling presence and power of the Holy Ghost. Do not be satisfied with a life that is not wholly swallowed up in God.

There are many books written on the Word, and we love clear, definite teaching on it, but go yourself to the Book and listen to what the Master says, and you will lay a sure foundation, that cannot be moved; for we are "begotten by the incorruptible Word of God." How we need that simplicity, that rest of faith, that brings us to the place where we are steadfast and immovable. Oh, the living Word of God! Can you not see that the Master was so interested in you that He could despise the shame, despise the cross? The judgment hall was nothing to Him; all the rebukes and scorn could not take from Him the joy of saving you and me. It was that joy that caused Him to say, "I count nothing too vile for Wigglesworth, I count nothing too vile for Brown, for *soul is on the wing to save the world!* How beautiful! How it should thrill us! He knew that death was represented in that sacred cup, and yet He joyfully said, "With desire - *I have a desire* to eat this passover with you before I suffer, Take the bread, drink of the cup, and as oft as ye take it, remember." In other words, take the memory of what it means home with you; think on it, analyze its meaning.

Jesus brought in a new creation by the words of His ministry. "No man born of woman is greater than John the Baptist, but the least in the *kingdom of Heaven* is greater than he" (Matthew 11:11). He said, "...the kingdom of God is within you" (Luke 17:21), and that He would "no more drink of the fruit of the vine until the Kingdom of God shall come" (Mark 14:25) and every person who has the new nature, the new birth, has the kingdom of God within them. If you believe God's Word, it will make you so live that the kingdom of God will be ever increasing, and the whole creation of the kingdom of God will be crying, "Come, Lord Jesus, Come!" and He will come.

As we come to the time of the breaking of bread, the thought should be, "How shall I partake of it?" Beloved, if before His death He could take it and say, "With desire I eat this passover with you before I suffer," we should be able to say, "Lord, I desire to eat it to please Thee, for I want my whole life to be on the wing for Thee!" What grace! As the stream of the new life begins to flow through your being, allow yourself to be immersed, carried on and on, with an ever-increasing flow, until your life becomes a ceaseless flow of the River of Life, and then it will be "No more I but Christ in me."

Get ready for the breaking of bread, and in doing so, "remember." Get ready for partaking of the wine, and in doing it, "Remember Him."

CHAPTER 9

Have Christians a Right to Pray "If It be Thy Will" Concerning Sickness?

By John G Lake

I AM GOING TO READ A FAMILIAR PORTION of the Word of God. It is the Lord's Prayer as recorded in the 11th chapter of Luke.

I purpose this afternoon to speak on this subject, "Have Christians a right to Pray, 'if it be Thy will' concerning sickness?" Personally, I do not believe they have, and I am going to give you my reasons.

> *And it came to pass that, as he was praying in a certain place, when He ceased, one of His disciples said unto Him, 'Lord, teach us to pray, as John taught his disciples.' And He said unto them, 'When ye pray, say, Our Father which art in heaven, hallowed be thy name. Thy kingdom come. Thy will be done as in heaven, so*

in earth. Give us day by day our daily bread. And forgive us our sins, for we also forgive everyone that is indebted to us. And lead us not into temptation; but deliver us from evil. —Luke 11:1-4

Beloved, if there is one thing in the world I wish I could do for the people of Spokane, it would be to teach them to pray. Not teach them to say prayers, but teach them, to pray. There is a mighty lot of difference between saying prayers and praying.

The prayer of faith shall save the sick, and the Lord shall raise him up, and if he have committed sins, they shall be forgiven him.

The prayer of faith has power in it. The prayer of faith has trust in it. The prayer of faith has healing in it for soul and body. The disciples wanted to know how to pray real prayers, and Jesus said unto them, "When ye pray say, Our Father which art in heaven ...Thy will be done."

Everybody stops there, and they resign their intelligence at that point to the unknown God. When you approach people and say to them, "You have missed the spirit of the prayer," they look at you in amazement. But, Beloved, it is a fact. I want to show it to you this afternoon as it is written in the Word of God. It does not say, "if it be Thy will," and stop there. There is a comma there, not a period. The prayer is this, "Thy will be done on earth as it is done in heaven." That is mighty different, is it not? Not "Thy will be done," let the calamity come, let my children be stricken with fever, or my son go to the insane asylum or my daughter go to the home of the feeble minded. That is not what Jesus was teaching the disciples to pray. Jesus was teaching the people to pray, "Thy will be done on earth as it is in heaven." Let the might of God be known. Let the power of God descend. Let God avert the calamity that is coming, Let it turn aside through faith in God. "Thy will be done on earth (here) as it is in heaven."

How is the will of God done in heaven? For a little time I want to direct your thought with mine heavenward. We step over there and we look all about the city. We note its beauty and its grandeur. We see the Lamb of God. We do not observe a single drunken man on the golden streets; not a single man on crutches; not a woman smelling of sin.

A man came in the other day and was telling me what an ardent Christian he is. But after he left, I said, "Lift the windows and let the balance of the man out." Men ought to smell like they pray. We defile ourselves with many things.

A dear man came to me the other day in great distress. He said his eyes were going blind. The physician told him he had only a year of sight, perhaps less. As I endeavoured to comfort him and turn his face toward God, I reverently put my hands on his eyes and asked God for Christ's sake to heal him, and as I did so the Spirit of God kept speaking to my soul and saying, "Amaurosis." I said, "What is amaurosis?" As soon as I could get to a dictionary, I looked up the word to see what it is. It is a disease of the eyes, caused by the use of nicotine. That was what was the matter with the man. The Spirit of the Lord was trying to tell me, but I was too dull; I did not understand. I do not know what the man's name is, but the other day God sent him back to my office. As we sat together I related the incident to him and said, "My brother, when you quit poisoning yourself the probability is that you may not need any healing from God."

We defile ourselves in various ways; we go on defiling ourselves; and some people are able to stand the defilement a long time and throw it off. Others are not able to. It poisons their system and destroys their faculties. One man may drink whisky and live to be an old man. Another may go to wreck in a few months or years. Some systems will throw off much; others will not.

Now, when we get to the beautiful City, we did not find any of these conditions, and so we say, "Angel, what is the reason you do not have any sin up here?"

"Why the reason we do not have any sin here is because the will of God is being done."

I have been used to looking for the sick, and if I see a man with a lame leg or a woman with a blind eye, I will see that a way-down the street. I have mingled with the sick all my life. So I look around up there, and I do not see anybody on crutches or anybody that is lame, no cancers or consumption, or any sickness at all. So I say to my guide, "Angel, tell me what the reason is that you do not have any sickness up here." The Angel replies, "The will of God is being done here." No sin where the will of God is being done. No sickness where the will of God is being done.

Then I return to the earth, and I can pray that prayer with a new understanding. "Thy will be done in me on earth as thy will is done in heaven." Just as the will of God is done there, so let the will of God be done here. Let the will of God be done in me. "Thy will be done, as in heaven, so in earth."

But someone says, "Brother, do you not remember on the 8th of Matthew how a leper came to Jesus one day and said to Him, "Lord, if Thou wilt, Thou canst make me clean?" The leper said, when he prayed, 'If it be Thy will,' why should I not say that too." Well, he was ignorant of what the will of Christ was concerning sickness. Perhaps he had been up on the mountainside and had heard Jesus preach that wonderful sermon on the mount, for it was at its close that he came to Jesus and said, "If thou wilt, thou canst make me clean." He knew Christ's ability to heal but did not understand his willingness. Jesus' reply settled the question for the leper and it should settle the question for every other man forever. Jesus said, "I will, be thou clean." If He ever had said anything else to any other man, there might be some reason for us to interject "if it be Thy will" in our prayers when we ask God for something He has declared His will on. "If" always doubts. The prayer of faith has no if's in it.

Suppose a drunken man kneels down at this platform and says, "I want to find God. I want to be a Christian." Every man and woman in this house who knows God would say, "Yes," right away. "Tell him to pray, to have faith in God, and God will deliver him." Why do you do it? Simply because there is no question in your mind concerning God's will in saving a sinner from his sins. You know He is ready to do it when a sinner is ready to confess his sin. But you take another step over, and here is another poor fellow by his side with a lame leg, and he comes limping along and kneels down, or tries to, and right away a lot of folks say, "I wish he would send for a doctor," or else pray, "if it be Thy will, make him well" forgetting "who forgiveth all thine iniquities, who healeth all thy diseases."

Instead of Christians taking the responsibility, they try to put the responsibility on God. Everything there is in the redemption of Jesus Christ is available for man when man will present his claim in faith and take it. There is no question in the mind of God concerning the salvation of a sinner. No more is there concerning the healing of the sick one. It is in the atonement of Jesus Christ, bless God. His atonement was unto the uttermost, to the last need of man. The responsibility rests purely, solely and entirely on man. Jesus put it there. Jesus said, "When ye pray, believe that ye receive, and ye shall have." No questions or if's in the words of Jesus. If He ever spoke with emphasis on any question, it was on the subject of God's will and the result of faith in prayer. Indeed, He did not even speak them in ordinary words, but in the custom of the East, He said, "Verily, verily." Amen, amen - the same as if I would stand in a American court and say, "I swear I will tell the truth, the whole truth, and nothing but the truth, so help me God." So the Easterner raised his hand and said, "Amen, amen." or "Verily, verily" - "with the solemnity of an oath I spy unto you." So Jesus said, "When ye pray, believe that ye receive, and ye shall have."

James, in expounding the subject, says concerning those that doubt, "Let not that man think that he shall receive anything of the Lord." Why? Well, he says, a man that doubteth is like a wave of the sea, driven with the wind and tossed. There is no continuity in his prayer. There is no continuity in his faith. There is no continuity in his character. There is no concentration in God for the thing that he wants. He is like the waves of the sea, scattered and shattered, driven here and there by the wind because there is "if" in it. "Let not that man think he shall receive anything of the Lord."

Now that leper did not know what the mind of Jesus was concerning sickness. Perhaps he had seen others healed of ordinary diseases, but leprosy was a terrible thing. It was incurable and contagious. The poor man was compelled as he went down the road to cry out, "Unclean, unclean," in order that people might run away from him.

In my work in South Africa I saw dozens of them, hundreds of them, thousands of them. I have seen them with their fingers off of the first joint, at the second joint, with their thumbs off, or nose off, their teeth gone, the toes off, the body scaling off, and I have seen God heal them in every stage. On one occasion in our work, a company of healed lepers gathered on Christmas eve and partook of the Lord's supper. Some had no fingers on their hands, and they had to take the cup between their wrists, but the Lord had been there and healed them. That was not under my ministry but under the ministry of a poor black fellow, who five or six years did not even wear pants. He wore a goat skin apron. But he came to Christ. He touched the living One. He received the power of God, and he manifests a greater measure of the real healing gift than I believe any man ever has in modern times. And if I were over there, I would kneel down and ask that black man to put his hands on my head and ask God to let the same power of God come into my life that he has in his.

You have no more right to pray "if it be Thy will" concerning your sickness than the leper had. Not as much, because for two thousand years the Word of God has been declared and the Bible has been an open book. We ought to be intelligent beyond any other people in the world concerning the mind of God.

"But Brother," someone says, "you have surely forgotten that when Jesus was in the garden He prayed 'Lord if it be possible, let this cup pass from me. Nevertheless, not as I will but as thou wilt.'" No, I have not forgotten. You are not the Saviour of the world, beloved. That was Jesus' prayer. No other man could ever pray that prayer but the Lord Jesus. But I want to show you, beloved, what caused Jesus to pray that prayer because a lot of folks have never understood it.

Jesus had gone into the garden to pray. The burden of His life was upon him. He was about to depart. He had a message for the world. He had been compelled to commit it to a few men - ignorant men. I believe that he wondered, "Will they be able to present the vision? Will they see it as I have seen it? Will they be able to let the people have it as I have given it to them?" No doubt, these were some of the inquiries besides many more.

Do you know what the spirit of intercession is? Do you

know what it means when a common man comes along, as Moses did, and takes upon himself the burden of the sin of the people and then goes down in tears and repentance unto God until the people are brought back in humility and repentance to His feet? When in anxiety for his race and people, Moses said, "Lord, if you forgive not this peoples blot my name out of thy book." He did not want any heaven where his people were not.

Think of it! Moses took upon himself that responsibility, and he said to God, "If you forgive not this people, blot my name out of thy book." God heard Moses' prayer, Bless God!

Paul, on one occasion, wrote practically the same words. "I would be accursed for my brethren, my kinsmen according to the flesh." He felt the burden of his people. So Jesus in the garden felt the burden of the world, the accumulated sorrows of mankind, their burdens of sin, their burdens of sickness. And as He knelt to pray, His heart breaking under it, the great drops of sweat came out on His brow like blood falling to the ground. But the critics have said, "It was not blood." Judge V. V. Barnes, in his great trial before Judge Landis, actually sweat blood until his handkerchief would be red with the blood that oozed through his pores. His wife said that for three months she was compelled to put napkins over his pillow. That is one of the biggest men God has ever let live in the world. His soul was big, and he saw the possibility of the hour for a great people and desired as far as he could to make that burden easy for them. He did not want the estate to go into the hands of a receiver. The interests of one hundred thousand people was in his hands, the accumulated properties of families who had no other resource. He was so large that the burden of his heart bore down on him so that he sweat blood and did so for three months. But people of these days say,

"It looked like blood," and are so teaching their Sunday School scholars. The Lord have mercy on them! The blood came out and fell down to the ground.

Jesus thought He was going to die right there in the garden, but He was too big to die there. He wanted to go to the cross. He wanted to see this thing finished on behalf of the race of man, and so He prayed, "Lord, if it be possible, let this cup pass from me. Nevertheless, not as I will, but as thou wilt." What was the cup? Was it the cup of suffering that was breaking Him down, that was draining the life blood out right then, and that would be His death instead of the cross? But He towered above that and prayed, "Lord, if it be possible, let this cup pass from me. Nevertheless, not as I will, but as thou wilt." Instantly the angels came and ministered to Him, and in the new strength He received, He went on to the cross and to His death as the Saviour of mankind.

Beloved, I want to tell you that if there was a little sweating of blood and that kind of prayer, there would be less sickness and sin than there is. God is calling for a people who will take upon them that kind of burden and let the power of God work through them.

People look in amazement in these days when God answers prayer for a soul. A week ago last night my dear wife and I went down to pray for a soul on the Fort Wright line, a Mrs. McFarland. She is going to be here one of these days to give her testimony. Ten years ago a tree fell on her and broke her back. She became paralysed, and for ten years she has been in a wheel chair, her limbs swollen, and her feet a great senseless lump that hangs down useless. She says many preachers have visited her in these years, and they have told her to be reconciled to the will of God, to sit still and suffer longer. She said, "Oh, I would not mind not walking; if the pain would just stop for a little while, it would be so good."

We lovingly laid our hands upon her and prayed. You say, "Did you pray, 'if it be Thy will?'" No! You bet I did not, but I laid my hands on that dear soul and prayed, "You devil that has been tormenting this woman for ten years and causing the tears to flow, I rebuke you in the Name of the Son of God. And by the authority of the Son of God I cast you out." Something happened. Life began to flow into her being, and the pain left. In a little while she discovered that power was coming back into her body. She called me up the other day and said, "Oh, such a wonderful thing has taken place. This morning in bed I could get up on my hands and knees." Poor soul, she called in her neighbours and relatives because she could get on her hands and knees in bed.

Do you not know you have painted Jesus Christ as a man without a soul? You have painted God as a tyrant. On the other hand, He is reaching out His hands in love to stricken mankind desiring to lift them up. But He has put the responsibility of the whole matter on you and me. That question of the will of God was everlastingly settled long ago, eternally settled, no question about the will of God.

The redemption of Jesus Christ was an uttermost redemption, to the last need of the human heart, bless God, for body, for soul, for spirit. He is a Christ and saviour even to the uttermost. Blessed be His Name. Who shall dare to raise a limit to the accomplishment of faith through Jesus Christ? I am glad the tendency is to take down the barriers and let all the faith of your heart go out to God for every man and for every condition of life, to let the love of God flow out of your soul to every hungry soul.

Instead of praying "Lord, if it be Thy will" when you kneel beside your sick friend, Jesus Christ has commanded you and every believer to lay your hands on the sick. This is not my ministry nor my brethren's only. It is the ministry of every believer. And if your ministers do not believe it, God have mercy on them; and if your churches do not believe it, God have mercy on them.

In these days the churches are screaming and crying because Christian-Science is swallowing up the world, and that it is false. Why do the people go to Christian Science? Because they cannot get any truth where they are. Let the day come when the voices of men ring out and tell the people the truth about the Son of God, who is a redeemer even unto the uttermost for body and soul and spirit. He redeems back to God. Beloved, believe it and receive the blessing that will come into your own life. Amen.

Printed in Great Britain
by Amazon